Lives of the Princesses of Wales

by Mary Beacock Fryer,
Arthur Bousfield,
and Garry Toffoli

Dundurn Press
Toronto and Charlottetown
1983

Acknowledgements

We wish to acknowledge the ongoing generous financial support of the **Canada Council** and the **Ontario Arts Council**.

Editor: Kirk Howard
Design and production: Ron and Ron Design Photography
Typesetting: Computype
Printing and binding: Laflamme & Charrier inc. Canada

Illustration and Photograph Acknowledgements

Ashley Lubin 77.
Colour Library International 4,12,21,29,44,69,72,76.
Duke of Buccleuch and Queensbury, K.T.,
  Boughton House, Kettering, England 16.
Guildhall Library, City of London 13,39,51,55.
High Commission of Australia 77.
High Commission of New Zealand 80.
High Commission of United Kingdom 74,75.
Illustrated London News 70.
Keystone Press Agency 66,67,78.
London Pictures Services 79.
Monarchy Canada 62, 69, 71
National Gallery 13.
National Portrait Gallery 10,20,24,28,32,35,36,37,40,43,45,47,48,52,53,
  56,60,61,64,68.

Published by
Dundurn Press Limited
P.O. Box 245, Station F
Toronto, Canada
M4Y 2L5

Canadian Cataloguing in Publication Data

Fryer, Mary Beacock, 1929-
  Lives of the Princesses of Wales

ISBN 0-919670-68-7 (bound). - ISBN 0-919670-69-5 (pbk.)

1. Great Britain - Princes and princesses - Biography.
I. Bousfield, Arthur, 1943-   II. Toffoli, Garry,
1953-   III. Title.

DA28.3.F79 1983   941'.009'92   C83-099238-3

Contents

The Prince and Princess of Wales on their wedding day at Buckingham Palace, 29 July 1983.

Introduction

This book is about nine lives — the lives of women who lived often widely separated in historic time but often within the same geographic space. All have known the old cities of London and Westminster, the very soul of England, the core of the primate city of the Commonwealth of Nations. These women lived under different conditions brought about by the passing of the centuries, but all have one thing in common. They are the Princesses of Wales. Their stories show how they coped with their unfolding roles in history, as people in their own right, not just as part of the wider histories of Princes of Wales and other sovereigns of Great Britain and the Commonwealth.

The title Prince of Wales can only be bestowed on the male heir who is first in line of succession to the throne of Great Britain and the Commonwealth monarchies.[1] The decision to create the heir Prince of Wales is made at the discretion of the reigning sovereign, who also has the right to decide when it will be awarded, and at what time the formal investiture will take place. A Princess of Wales is the wife of a Prince of Wales. Where a woman is first in the line of succession she is not created Princess of Wales. The title is a courtesy one, that applies only to a Prince of Wales' consort, and her official title is Princess of Wales preceded by her first name, unless she is herself born a Princess in her own right.

The titles originated during the lifetime of King Edward I (1239 – 1307) who ascended the throne of England in 1272. This King had ambitions to create one island kingdom by annexing Wales and Scotland. He died still struggling to unite Scotland with England, but he was more successful against Wales. Edward began his campaign against the Welsh in 1277. By 1282 he had succeeded, and he decided to make Wales a principality subordinate to the English Crown. In 1284, to placate the Welsh nobles, Edward offered them as their own prince, according to legend, one who spoke neither English nor French.

The nobles accepted, confident the King would offer them a Welshman. Edward presented them with his own infant son, the future Edward II, who had been born at Carnaervon, Wales. At the time the heir was too young to speak any language at all. Thus Edward I's son became the first Prince of Wales, although he was not formally invested with the title until 1301 when he was seventeen years old. Some time would pass before there was a Princess of Wales. The first Prince did not marry until after he became King in 1307.

Since the time when Edward I decided that the heir to the throne could be created Prince of Wales, England, her expanding Empire, and now the Commonwealth monarchies have had thirty-three sovereigns who have reigned for varying lengths of time. The shortest reign was that of Lady Jane Grey (from whose sister, Lady Katherine Grey, our present Princess of Wales is descended). Lady Jane reigned nine days in 1553. Counted as one reign was that of William III and Mary II, who ruled jointly. Mary inherited the throne when her father, King James II, was deposed in 1688, at which time she was the consort of the Dutch ruler, Prince William of Orange. William accepted the throne on condition that he reign as King, rather than as Mary's consort. In fact, he was King until his death in 1702, although Mary predeceased him in 1694.

From the foregoing, it is apparent that not all the sovereigns were Princes of Wales before ascending the throne. All told, seven monarchs in their own right were women. As well, certain of the men did not succeed through the direct line. Nor did all the Princes of Wales ascend the throne; six predeceased their fathers, and one, James, the son of the deposed James II, grew up in exile.

According to the official record, there have been twenty-one Princes of Wales. (Not counted is Henry Tudor, son of Henry VIII and Katharine of Aragon, created Prince of Wales when a few days old and dead within two months). And these twenty-one Princes of Wales have had only nine Princess consorts. While Prince Charles is the twenty-first Prince of Wales, he will be only the fourteenth to ascend the throne. His consort, Lady Diana Spencer, is our ninth Princess of Wales, but she will be the seventh to become Queen. Considering that the title spans 700 years, this averages only one woman per century who was both Princess of Wales and Queen consort. Furthermore, two of the Princesses of Wales — Lady Anne Neville and Katharine of Aragon — became Queen through later marriages and were not consorts of Princes of Wales at the time of their coronations. Lady Anne Neville, widow of Edward, the fifth Prince of Wales, was the Queen consort of Richard III; Katharine of Aragon, widow of Arthur, the eighth Prince of Wales, was the consort of Henry VIII. One Princess of Wales, Caroline of Brunswick, whose husband ascended the throne as George IV, was not crowned with him.

The title Princess of Wales is a rare one in the annals of the British royal family. In a very real sense, each woman who has held the title was a product of her own era. Until the nineteenth century, among royal families, marriages were arranged for political reasons or expediency. Love and compatability were secondary considerations. Marriages between future monarchs and their consorts were used to strengthen alliances, to achieve a balance of power. By the eighteenth century, German princesses were useful consorts for heirs to the British throne. Discouraged were marriages with powerful members of the native nobility, which might invite jealousies and charges of favouritism from other great families. For Britain,

Germany, then divided into many kingdoms, principalities and duchies, offered the prospect of a consort without vested interests who would be neutral. In practice neutrality was apt to be a myth; such imported consorts readily joined or led factions.

Becoming a Princess of Wales could be a very lonely business, especially at first. Of the nine Princesses, five were from foreign countries, and for them English was not their mother tongue. In addition to having to master a new language efficiently, these Princesses had to combat homesickness and alien customs, not to mention the rigours of the British climate. Of the foreign Princesses, three arrived in London for the first time, already committed to marriages with husbands they had never seen. They could not back out once they found themselves in strange surroundings. For the other two, Alexandra of Denmark and Caroline of Ansbach, the transition was less traumatic. Alexandra had met her future husband in advance. Caroline had been married to hers for several years, and she probably made the easiest adjustment of all. The foreign Princesses shared one alleviating circumstance; all had known from childhood that they were destined to marry rulers, and to do so they would have to go to courts that were exotic to them.

For the earliest consorts a most vital function was producing heirs to the throne to secure the succession, an especially crucial role in times when infant mortality was high, life-expectancy short — conditions overcome only recently by enlightened pre-natal care, improved nutrition and sophisticated medical knowledge. Today the royal family is healthier than it has ever been, with a line of succession that would have been the envy of earlier generations. Katharine of Aragon's health was adversely affected by the many pregnancies she underwent that resulted in only one healthy child. Queen Anne bore seventeen children, of which only one, Prince William Duke of Gloucester, lived any length of time, and he died at age eleven.

Perhaps the greatest change that has taken place in the selection of consorts has been that from arranged marriages to cement alliances to a choice of a partner who could be called merely suitable. This greater freedom of choice has parallelled the evolution of the sovereign from one who wielded considerable political power to one who reigns by influence and limited power though remaining the source of authority.

The first such suitable marriage appears to have been that of Albert Edward (Edward VII) heir to Queen Victoria, and Princess Alexandra of Denmark. While a little contrived, that marriage was agreeable to both partners and of no political advantage to Britain.

When in 1864 Austria and Prussia decided to annex the Danish duchies of Schleswig and Holstein, Queen Victoria's government refused to take sides. Alexandra was bereft when her adopted country refused to come to the aid of her native land.

Even more suitable was the marriage of Princess Mary of Teck to the Duke of York, later Prince of Wales and George V. Although the couple were devoted to each other, George the sailor Prince, was far too dutiful a man to contemplate a marriage that would not invoke widespread public approval. The reverse was true of George V's heir, the twentieth Prince of Wales and later Edward VIII. The woman he loved, and for whom he gave up his throne in December 1936 was Mrs. Wallis Warfield Simpson, twice-divorced with two living husbands. Gone were the days of Joan of Kent, the first Princess of Wales, when a papal dispensation could overcome the obstacle posed by a living husband. Mrs. Simpson, in a word, was not suitable. Many of Edward's subjects and his government rejected her, amidst the most glaring publicity to which, until that time, the royal family had ever been exposed.

Many Britons felt that a King who was head of the Church of England, which at that time did not recognize divorce, could not have as his consort a woman whose background precluded her participation in the ritual of that church. Most people in the then Dominions felt the same way, while Canada had an added cause for concern. She was an American, and anti-Americanism lay at the core of Canadian nationalism. The two sovereigns who have followed Edward VIII have showed themselves very aware that the future of a constitutional monarchy rests on its popularity. This has been borne out by the way in which the present monarch and her consort have handled the upbringing of the heir, in the conduct of the heir himself, and in his choice of a consort.

Charles, the eldest son of Queen Elizabeth II and her consort, Prince Philip Duke of Edinburgh, was created Prince of Wales on 26 July 1958 when he was nine years old. His investiture, held in the castle at Carnaervon, did not take place until the summer of 1969 when he reached age twenty. Investitures have not always been held in public, nor at Carnaervon. The custom was revived in 1911 on the recommendation of Lloyd George, then the Chancellor of the Exchequer, for the investiture of Edward the twentieth Prince of Wales (Edward VIII). Lloyd George, himself a Welshman, suggested that holding the investiture at Carnaervon would impress upon the Welsh people that Edward was indeed their own Prince.

Amidst a strengthening of nationalist sentiments among some of the Welsh, Queen Elizabeth II decided that Carnaervon was the most appropriate place for the investiture of her heir. In preparation for the ceremony, Prince Charles went a step further than his predecessor, by learning to speak some Welsh. Not surprisingly, one of the first important visits made by the present Prince and Princess of Wales following their wedding was to the principality to show the Welsh people that to them, they are very special.

In the two years that have passed since their marriage, the new Waleses have exhibited incredible energy and endurance. Apart from finding the time to produce a future Prince of Wales, their days have been crowded with public appearances. They have also made an extensive tour of Australia and New Zealand, with their son Prince William accompanying them, and a shorter one to Canada. As well, many people have glimpsed them on private visits to the Caribbean and other places.

Of course His Royal Highness has been a world traveller for many years whose tours have been avidly watched by both the public and the press. While no one would suggest that the world is tired of seeing him, everyone wants to be introduced to the young woman who has joined what Prince Philip calls "the family firm". With Lady Diana sharing her husband's spotlight, royal tours have taken on a new glamour — an understatement. Prince Charles might well echo the words of the late President John F. Kennedy, when he observed: "I'm the man who accompanied Jacqueline Kennedy to Paris".

Books about the royal family are legion; there are several on the Princes of Wales. At the time of writing, a spate of volumes has appeared about Diana, Princess of Wales, and she has become known, popularly and inaccurately, as Princess Diana. While some books include references to her predecessors, there has not been a book especially devoted to recounting the lives of all the women who have been Princesses of Wales. Some of their stories show similarities; some are sad. But their lives are as varied as the times in which they have lived. A common thread running through all nine lives is the appalling demands the role has thrust upon them. These range from the trauma of arriving, sight-unseen, in a new country, through political intrigue and a struggle for self-preservation, to the more recent glare of publicity that wreaks havoc with privacy.

1. Antigua and Barbuda, Australia, Bahamas, Barbados, Belize, Canada, St Christopher and Nevis, Fiji, Grenada, Jamaica, Mauritius, New Zealand, Papua New Guinea, St Lucia, St Vincent and Grenadines, Solomon Islands and Tuvalu.

Joan of Kent
1328 – 1385

The first woman to become a Princess of Wales was Joan Plantagenet, later known as the Fair Maid of Kent. She was the consort of Edward Prince of Wales, the heir to King Edward III, but she never became Queen. During Joan's lifetime three important historic events occurred. The backdrop to her story was the Hundred Years' War, from 1337 to 1453, the age when the Plantagenet monarchs of England claimed the throne of France and made many attempts to secure it. Closer to home were, first, the Black Death of 1348 – 1349, which reduced the able-bodied people of England, causing a labour shortage. The second was the Peasants' Revolt of 1381, a consequence of the Black Death. Without the labour shortage the latter created, which raised expectations amongst the rural masses, the peasantry might never have attempted to improve their lot through rebellion.

Edward, heir to King Edward III, was the second man to be created Prince of Wales, but he was better known as the Black Prince. Like his Princess, Edward was tall and fair, and his nickname derived from the black armour he wore in battle. The marriage of Edward the Black Prince and Joan of Kent was a happy one, and an unusual match for the time. That they became husband and wife in an era when arranged unions between royal houses were customary, is a tribute to their strong-willed Plantagenet blood.

As her nickname implies, the Fair Maid of Kent was attractive, but for many years she was not considered a suitable bride for Edward. A union with Joan would not yield any advantages for the country. Born in 1328, she was the third of four children of Edmund Earl of Kent and Margaret Wake of Liddell, Cumberland. Their home was Arundel Castle in Hampshire. By the time Joan was two years old, tragedy had engulfed her family. The sad event was triggered by the clandestine murder of King Edward II, at the instigation of his own Queen Isabella of France. In 1327 the King was deposed and he vanished. Joan's father, Edmund Earl of Kent, was Edward II's much younger half-brother. Worried over the fate of his elder half-brother, Edmund began investigating the circumstances of his disappearance and subsequent murder.

An infuriated Queen Isabella, without the knowledge of her son, now Edward III, arranged to have Edmund charged with treason. Soldiers seized Arundel Castle and held Edmund's wife and children prisoner. At that time Margaret Countess of Kent had two children, Margaret and Joan, and was carrying another. On 16 March 1330, Edmund Earl of Kent was executed at Windsor. A month later his countess gave birth to a son she named John.

When Edward III became aware of the injustice done to his uncle, he banished his mother to East Anglia. Edward III's Queen, Philippa of Hainaut, set

Effigy of Edward, Prince of Wales, the 'Black Prince', at Canterbury Cathedral.

out to make amends. The Kent family was freed and brought to court, then the palace of Woodstock, north of Oxford, so that the dead earl's children could be raised in the royal nursery. Queen Philippa was herself pregnant when Margaret Countess of Kent arrived with her children. Before the year ended, an infant Black Prince had joined his first-cousins, once removed, in the nursery at Woodstock. Thus Joan and Edward were brought up together under the watchful eye of Queen Philippa.

Each child was assigned a governor and governess. Joan's were William and Catherine Montague, 1st Earl and Countess of Salisbury. This enterprising couple decided that Joan would wed their own son William. The Fair Maid of Kent had other ideas, which for a time complicated her life. In 1340 when she was only twelve years old she fell in love with Thomas Holland, eight years her senior and a steward in the Salisbury household. They contracted a marriage by swearing their love before witnesses, legal at that time but not in the opinion of the Salisburys. The following year, while Thomas Holland was abroad fighting in one of the many campaigns of the Hundred Years' War, Joan's governor and governess forced her to marry William, the future 2nd Earl of Salisbury.

When Thomas returned from France he could do little to reclaim his wife, for he had powerful opponents, and he soon went off on other campaigns, serving with the Black Prince at the Battle of Crécy in 1346. Meanwhile, back at court, Joan was being addressed as the Countess of Salisbury, since the 1st Earl had died in 1344. She was now a great favourite of King Edward III. While the French town of Calais was under siege in 1347 – 1348, Queen Philippa and other ladies joined the King there. At a ball occurred the famous incident where a lady dropped her garter. Edward III said, "Honi soit qui mal y pense", and resolved to create his new order of chivalry — the Order of the Garter. Although legend suggested that the Queen had dropped her garter, the story is also associated with Joan, the beautiful young Countess of Salisbury.

Meanwhile, Thomas Holland, who had not forgotten Joan, was winning battle honours. Among the first men created Knights of the Garter were the Black Prince and Thomas Holland, Joan's true love. Wealthy after helping plunder large areas of France, Sir Thomas Holland appealed to Pope Clement VI to arrange Joan's divorce from Salisbury. In 1348 the court was at Otford, near Sevenoaks, Kent, and it included Joan, her two "husbands", and the Black Prince, who gave his cousin "Jeanette" a silver "biker".

That same year the Black Death ravaged the land, and the population of England was reduced from

10

four million to two and one half million. The following year the plague eased, and for Joan there was contentment. In November 1348 the Pope decided in favour of Sir Thomas Holland's claim and Joan returned to him. During the years when she had been officially Salisbury's wife, she had no children, but once she was with Holland she soon became a mother.

All told, Joan bore Holland three sons and two daughters. Her eldest son was Thomas, a second son Edmund died young, and the third was John. Her cousin the Black Prince was godfather to Joan's two surviving sons. By 1353 Joan and Sir Thomas had become the Earl and Countess of Kent. Joan's mother Margaret, sister Margaret and brother John had all predeceased her, leaving her substantial property. But her happy marriage ended with Sir Thomas' death in December 1360.

Joan, now thirty-two years old, was a very eligible prize — for any man but the Prince of Wales. Suitors flocked around the wealthy widow in hopes of a favourable response to their entreaties, but Joan seemed immune. The most ardent sought out the Black Prince, begging him to intercede for them with his still beautiful though now stout cousin. Edward declined to involve himself in Joan's life, until one whom he could not refuse approached him. Sir Denis Brocas, a knight in Edward's own entourage, beseeched the Prince to assist him, and Edward agreed to act as the go-between.

Joan refused to consider Brocas and dissolved in tears. She declared that her heart was already pledged to "the most chivalrous Knight under heaven", who was unattainable. Edward, greatly touched by the tears, pressed her to identify this paragon. Joan played her cards correctly, and admitted her love for her cousin, who resolved to make her his consort. The timing was perfect, which Joan probably suspected. Edward III and Philippa, while not pleased with their son's choice, acquiesced. The Prince of Wales was thirty years old, and if he were ever to have a legitimate heir he should not procrastinate much longer.

Joan had proved that she was fertile, and so had the Black Prince. Although the Prince's main interest had been the Plantagenet claim to the throne of France, he had sired at least three natural sons. Once King Edward and Queen Philippa gave their consent to the marriage, a papal dispensation was necessary. The 2nd Earl of Salisbury was still living; the Black Prince was godfather to Joan's two sons; they were also first-cousins. The Pope sent the dispensation, and the marriage took place in October 1361 at Westminster Abbey.

The Black Prince owned several residences, Wallingford Castle, Kennington, a house in London, and

The Black Prince tells Joan the story of the Battle of Poitiers in a curious 18th Century portrayal of the royal couple wearing classical instead of Medieval dress.

The Medieval Tower of London. During the Peasants' Revolt the mob invaded Joan's apartments here, causing her to flee secretly.

11

Arundel Castle, Sussex, Joan's earliest home.

Garter procession at Windsor Castle 1965. Joan's father-in-law King Edward III rebuilt Windsor as the home of his new order of chivalry. According to legend Joan was the lady whose garter the King retrieved.

The Wilton diptych shows Joan's youthful son King Richard II kneeling in adoration before the Madonna and Child.

Angels carry the cross of St George, patron of the Order of the Garter.

Richard II aged 14 calms the rebels in 1381. His mother awaited the outcome of this daring foray in her quarters at the Tower.

Berkhamsted in Hertfordshire. The latter was his favourite home, and there the newly-weds went to stay, but not for very long. The Prince was anxious to return to France to secure more territory. Having the heir occupied abroad suited the King, for a Prince of Wales in England was apt to become the centre of plots to depose the monarch. Bordeaux would make a fine headquarters for the Black Prince and Joan — at a safe distance from the court.

In February 1362 the couple sailed for France accompanied by Joan's children, and landed at La Rochelle. Two years later, while staying at Angoêuleme, north of Bordeaux, Joan gave birth to a son they named Edward. The Black Prince was delighted. Late in 1366, the Prince was anxious to go campaigning but he postponed leaving Bordeaux for Joan was again pregnant. On 6 January 1367 a second son named Richard was born. Once he was assured that Joan had recovered, the Prince set out for the south, to check an advance over the Pyrenees by a Spanish army.

On his return to Bordeaux the Prince was far from well. His younger brother the Duke of Lancaster, better known as John of Gaunt, joined him and carried on the campaign. In January 1371, Prince Edward, aged six years, died, and his parents were grief stricken. With Joan and young Richard the Black Prince sailed for England, leaving John of Gaunt to arrange for the child's funeral. The family resumed residence at Berkhamsted, but the Black Prince's health grew steadily worse.

As he became more and more ill, the Prince fretted over the succession, suspicious that John of Gaunt would claim the throne on the death of Edward III. Richard was first in the succession, and while primogeniture was established it was not hard and fast. Between the Prince of Wales and John of Gaunt was another brother, Lionel Duke of Clarence, whose daughter Philippa, also took precedence over John of Gaunt. The Black Prince feared that both his baby son and Lionel's daughter might be set aside by John of Gaunt. He wondered, too, whether Joan's earlier marriages might be used as an excuse to have Richard declared illegitimate, but he was reckoning without his forceful wife. While the Black Prince had been strong Joan did not involve herself in politics, but she showed no small skill when the future of her son might be in jeopardy.

On 25 January 1376, Richard was to appear before Parliament. King Edward III was failing fast, and with the Black Prince also near death the members wanted to see whether the small heir seemed capable of fulfilling the destiny that awaited him. Joan saw that her son was dressed plainly so that his clothing would not detract from his good looks and bearing. Parliament was impressed by the child, and ordered that Richard be created Prince of Wales as soon as the Black Prince died. The latter succumbed in June when Richard was nine years old. The body lay in state at Westminster Hall, London, until 30 September, when it was taken to Canterbury and buried in the Cathedral. As Parliament had decreed, Richard was made Prince of Wales on 20 November 1376.

At age forty-eight and stouter than ever, the Fair Maid of Kent was again a widow, with a mission to protect the future King Richard II. When the boy was created Prince of Wales, the ambitions of John of Gaunt were dealt a severe blow. Yet Joan intended to maintain a cordial relationship with her brother-in-law for the sake of her son.

In June 1377 Edward III died, and a mob of Londoners marched to attack John of Gaunt. Joan hid him at Kennington, a shrewd move to place the ambitious Duke of Lancaster under an obligation to the Black Prince's widow and heir. As Joan hoped, Richard was crowned on 16 July. A council ruled during the new King's minority, and he remained in Joan's care. The Fair Maid was in effect head of the court, and popular with the people. She made certain she had a foot in two camps, that of Richard II, and of his uncle John of Gaunt.

One thing that eased the tension between them was their mutual interest in the teachings of John Wycliffe, who favoured a measure of independence for the Church in England from the Pope in Rome. Some of the clergy viewed Wycliffe's opinions as sheer heresy. John of Gaunt has been credited with safeguarding Wycliffe so that he was able to die a natural death. The Dowager Princess of Wales was another good friend to Wycliffe, possibly because she found it politic to side with John of Gaunt for Richard's sake.

For the next few years Joan was the most formidable person at court, a situation she recognized as temporary. Richard needed a wife, and by 1379 negotiations were being conducted for a betrothal with Princess Anne of Bohemia, one year older than the boy-king. Thomas Holland, Richard's older half-brother, travelled between London and Prague working out the details.

In 1381 the peasants rose in revolt. An army of rebel peasants marched towards Canterbury, looking for the Archbishop, who was then with King Richard in the Tower of London. The Dowager Princess of Wales had chosen this dangerous time to be returning from a pilgrimage to the Black Prince's tomb. Now too plump to ride a palfrey Joan was travelling in a heavy carriage. Near Blackheath her conveyance became mired in mud and her servants were not strong enough to free it.

The mob overtook Joan's party, and good-naturedly hauled the carriage free. According to legend, the bolder peasants kissed the beloved Fair Maid of Kent. As her carriage resumed the journey, the mob called after her, "For King Richard and the true Commons". Joan reached London Bridge well ahead of the rebels and reported what she had seen of the uprising to her son and his advisers in the Tower.

On 13 June the mob entered London, sacked and burned John of Gaunt's palace, the Savoy, and surrounded the Tower. Fourteen-year-old Richard and an escort set out to parlay with the rebels. During the King's absence the drawbridge was left down in case he needed to make a hasty retreat. Joan was nearly beside herself out of fear for Richard's safety, but before his return those inside the Tower seemed in greater peril. Some of the mob invaded the Tower and entered Joan's own chamber. Her maids dressed her and had her rowed up the Thames to an inconspicuous building known as the Wardrobe. Meanwhile, Richard finished his negotiations with the rebels and hurried to join his mother. She was so relieved to see him that she was close to hysterics.

On the advice of his council, Richard repudiated some concessions he had made, and the rebellion was supressed brutally. This was but the first occasion when Richard was to prove a weak King, a failing that would ultimately lead to his downfall, but not until long after Joan was dead.

When life returned to normal, the arrangements for Richard's marriage were concluded. Escorted by the King's half-brother John Holland, Anne of Bohemia arrived in England and the marriage ceremony took place on 14 January 1382 in St. Stephen's Chapel, Westminster. Soon afterwards Joan retired to Wallingford, but she did not remain uninvolved. Richard was a peaceloving, artistic youth who lacked the warlike qualities necessary in a successful fourteenth century monarch. These were present in abundance in John of Gaunt, and Joan felt compelled to continue as peacemaker between the young King and his grasping uncle. She made many journeys in her carriage from Wallingford to Pontefract Castle, John of Gaunt's stronghold in Yorkshire, to reconcile uncle and nephew.

The 300 kilometre journey grew increasingly taxing as Joan's limbs became less and less able to bear her weight. In her carriage the journey took three weeks, and she slept at her various manors going and coming. She was able to keep John of Gaunt on Richard's side by pointing out to him certain hard facts. While many in the country would have been happy to see Richard deposed, this particular uncle was very unpopular with both the aristocracy and the masses, and could never hope to succeed the boy-king.

At the end of her life, Joan was disturbed by dissent between two of her sons. In 1385 a French army landed in Scotland. Richard, now eighteen, led an English army north, accompanied by his uncles and his half-brother John Holland. That headstrong young man felt himself above the law. Passing through Yorkshire, one of John Holland's squires was attacked by an archer in the train of Hugh, Earl of Stafford. In retaliation Holland ran his sword through Ralph, Hugh's eldest son, and killed him. Stafford sent a message to Richard accusing Holland of wanton murder. Suspecting that many nobles would desert him with their trains if he did nothing, Richard decided to punish his half-brother.

On discovering that Richard intended to have him arrested, Holland fled to the sanctuary of the Church of St. John of Beverley. When the news reached Wallingford, Joan sent messages north begging Richard to be merciful to his half-brother for their mother's sake. The strain proved too much for the Dowager Princess of Wales, now fragile at age fifty-seven. She died in August while Richard's army was crossing into Scotland, without knowing the fate of John Holland.

Joan the Fair Maid of Kent was buried, not near the Black Prince in Canterbury Cathedral, but beside her first husband, Sir Thomas Holland, in the Church of the Friars Minor at Stamford, Lincolnshire. She did not live to see that Richard treated his half-brother John leniently as she had wished. The only penalty he exacted was an order for John to provide chantries where Masses could be said for the soul of Ralph of Stafford. Richard was generous, too, to his elder half-brother Thomas, who became the Earl of Kent and was allowed to inherit most of their mother's property.

Joan of Kent, the first Princess of Wales, was a strong character who had considerable influence in the years after the Black Prince died. She did not live to witness the tragedy that overcame her youngest son. Fourteen years later, in 1399, John of Gaunt's son, known as Henry Bolingbroke, deposed Richard II. The following year the imprisoned King was either murdered outright or allowed to starve to death. Richard was a misfit in the age of warrior kings. Perhaps the Fair Maid of Kent understood her son better than he did himself.

Lady Anne Neville

1456 – 1485

The second Princess of Wales was Anne, the younger daughter of Richard Neville, Earl of Salisbury and Warwick (1428 – 1571), nicknamed "The King-maker". Anne is best remembered as the wife of King Richard III, but before their marriage she was the consort of Edward Prince of Wales, the son of Henry VI. Like the Black Prince, the husband of Joan the first Princess of Wales, Edward never became King.

Anne lived during the Wars of the Roses (1455 – 1485), a civil strife between two rival houses for the throne. The House of Lancaster, represented by Henry VI and his son Edward, consisted of descendants of John of Gaunt, the Duke of Lancaster, a man well known to the first Princess of Wales. The symbol of the Lancastrians was the red rose. Opposing them were the descendants of John of Gaunt's brother, Edmund Duke of York, who chose as their badge the white rose. As a daughter of the Kingmaker, Anne Neville was destined to be offered to each side — and to be accepted. By the first alliance, with the House of Lancaster, Anne was Princess of Wales; by the second, with the House of York, she was Queen.

Not much is known about Anne Neville until she was fifteen; and afterwards her story became intertwined with that of Richard III. His character was blackened in Tudor times, when chroniclers gave one version, aided by Shakespeare. In recent times historians have looked at pre-Tudor documents and have concluded that Richard exercised poor judgement but he was by no means the arch villian of the Tudor accounts. Now a Richard III Society has been formed whose purpose is to rehabilitate the maligned King. In the Tudor and modern versions, two quite different Anne Nevilles emerge. While the Richard III Society may be over-generous with whitewash, their version is probably closer to the truth. The following facts are known about Anne Neville's early life.

She was born at Warwick Castle on 11 June 1456. Her mother was Anne Beauchamp, whose father was the 13th Earl of Warwick, and whose only brother Henry inherited the title as the 14th Earl, but he died in 1447. Anne Beauchamp became the Countess of Warwick because there was no male heir, and two years later her husband, Richard Neville, 2nd Earl of Salisbury, was created 15th Earl of Warwick in his wife's right. (The first Princess of Wales, Joan of Kent, was a Countess of Salisbury, but in the interval the title had died out and been revived.)

The combined wealth of the Beauchamp and Neville families was considerable. Anne Beauchamp inherited Warwick Castle, while Richard Neville fell heir to Middleham Castle in Yorkshire from his father, the 1st Earl of Salisbury. Anne Beauchamp was not strong, and she had only two children, Anne, the future Princess of Wales, and Isabel, five years older. Because Richard Neville was a Warden of the West

Marches, responsible for keeping the peace along the Scottish border, the family spent more time at Middleham than at Warwick. Middleham was the more comfortable home, and there Anne and her sister Isabel spent a happy childhood.

In the early stages of the Wars of the Roses, the Earl of Warwick supported the Yorkist faction. In 1461 he helped depose John of Gaunt's great grandson Henry VI, who was confined in the Tower of London, and to place Edmund of York's great grandson, Edward IV, on the throne. By 1470 Warwick was quarrelling with Edward IV, because he disliked the way Edward's Queen, Elizabeth Woodville, was advancing the interests of her relatives. Fearing the vengeance of the King and the Woodvilles, Warwick fled to France, where he formed an alliance with Margaret of Anjou, Henry VI's Queen. Warwick led an army to England and released Henry VI in September 1470, and in turn Edward IV fled to the continent. Next, Edward rallied the Yorkists and returned to England. The Kingmaker's career ended with his death at the Battle of Barnet in the spring of 1471.

When he was supporting the Yorkists, the Earl of Warwick had married his elder daughter, Isabel, to George Duke of Clarence, a younger brother of Edward IV and elder brother of Richard Duke of Gloucester, the future Richard III. After his quarrel with Edward IV and flight to France, Warwick decided to marry his younger daughter Anne to Edward Prince of Wales, the son of Henry VI, the Lancastrian King. Either the Duke of Clarence or Edward Prince of Wales might become King, and one of his daughters would be a Queen.

Edward Prince of Wales was born at Westminster in 1453. Because of King Henry VI's periodic lapses into madness, at the insistence of Queen Margaret, Edward was created Prince of Wales when still a baby. He led a short, chaotic life in the Lancastrian-Yorkist tug-of-war. In 1463 at age ten he was taken to Scotland for safety. Then the Queen managed to reach France with her son, where the Earl of Warwick joined them. In 1470 he had Anne Neville brought there to be betrothed to Edward. The ceremony took place in the cathedral of Angers, and the couple took their oaths on a piece of the True Cross. At that time Anne was fourteen, her future husband seventeen.

Historians agree on the time and place of the betrothal, but are less certain that a marriage took place. Some sources suggest that no record survives; others claim that the marriage was solemnized in December 1470. Whichever is correct, a betrothal was such a serious matter at the time that Anne Neville may be considered a true Princess of Wales.

Soon after the betrothal, the Earl of Warwick and the Duke of Clarence crossed into England with an army, and Edward IV fled to Burgundy. Henry VI was released from the Tower of London and reinstated as King. On learning of Warwick's successes, Queen Margaret set out with her son and Anne for England and they landed at Weymouth on 14 April 1471. Henry VI's restoration was short-lived, for Edward IV had arrived back in England ahead of Queen Margaret. On the day that the Queen, Edward and Anne went ashore at Weymouth, Edward IV defeated the Earl of Warwick at the Battle of Barnet in which the latter was slain. Henry VI was once more a prisoner of Edward IV. To save himself the Duke of Clarence made peace with his elder brother Edward IV.

Margaret of Anjou rallied supporters in the West Country and her Lancastrian army met a superior Yorkist force at Tewkesbury, in Gloucestershire on 3 May. The following day the forces of Edward IV and his brother, Richard Duke of Gloucester, inflicted a crushing defeat on those of Queen Margaret. Edward Prince of Wales was killed, or murdered afterwards. Margaret and Anne took refuge in a nearby church, where the Yorkists found them. Queen Margaret was taken to London and confined in the Tower, where her husband was already a prisoner. Anne was made a ward of her sister's husband, George Duke of Clarence. That much of Anne Neville's story is straightforward, and historians are in agreement. At this point the Tudor minions and the moderns diverge.

The Tudor Version

Following the Battle of Tewkesbury the stage was set for infighting amongst the victorious members of the House of York. The first to recount the period were the chroniclers serving Richard III's successor, Henry VII. On their portrait of a murderous, deformed Richard, William Shakespeare wrote his stirring drama of the sadistic, hunch-backed King who got his just deserts later on Bosworth field. Of course the dramatist followed the gospel according to the Tudors, since he wrote King Richard III in 1592 – 1593, a decade before the death of Elizabeth I, the last Tudor monarch.

Shakespeare agreed that Richard III had his nephews, the boy King Edward V and his younger brother Prince Richard Duke of York, confined in the Tower of London and murdered. The bard shows Anne Neville, the widow of Edward Prince of Wales, who incidently was murdered by Richard, as the reluctant bride of this villain. Tudor chroniclers further accused Richard of conspiring to poison Anne, in order to be free to marry Elizabeth of York, a daughter of Edward IV (and his own niece) after his only son died.

The events surrounding Richard's marriage to Anne were also distorted. Following the Battle of

Great seal of Richard III.

What happened to the Prince of Wales? The death of Anne's first husband after Tewkesbury remains a mystery. This picture of the Prince being brought before Edward IV reflects the Tudor story that he was killed by the King's brother, Richard.

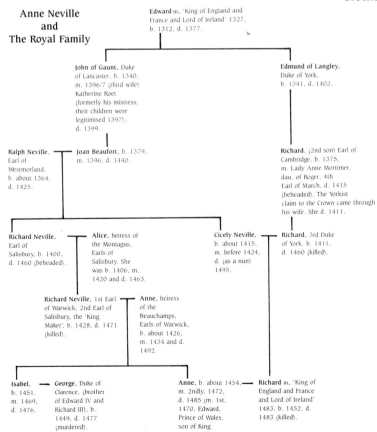

Anne Neville and The Royal Family

Edward III, 'King of England and France and Lord of Ireland' 1327, b. 1312, d. 1377.

John of Gaunt, Duke of Lancaster, b. 1340, m. 1396/7 (third wife) Katherine Roet (formerly his mistress; their children were legitimised 1397), d. 1399.

Edmund of Langley, Duke of York, b. 1341, d. 1402.

Ralph Neville, Earl of Westmorland, b. about 1364, d. 1425.

Joan Beaufort, b. 1379, m. 1396, d. 1440.

Richard, (2nd son) Earl of Cambridge, b. 1375, m. Lady Anne Mortimer, dau. of Roger, 4th Earl of March, d. 1415 (beheaded). The Yorkist claim to the Crown came through his wife. She d. 1411.

Richard Neville, Earl of Salisbury, b. 1400, d. 1460 (beheaded).

Alice, heiress of the Montagus, Earls of Salisbury. She was b. 1406, m. 1420 and d. 1463.

Cicely Neville, b. about 1415, m. before 1424, d. (as a nun) 1495.

Richard, 3rd Duke of York, b. 1411, d. 1460 (killed).

Richard Neville, 1st Earl of Warwick, 2nd Earl of Salisbury, the 'King Maker', b. 1428, d. 1471 (killed).

Anne, heiress of the Beauchamps, Earls of Warwick, b. about 1426, m. 1434 and d. 1492.

Isabel, b. 1451, m. 1469, d. 1476.

George, Duke of Clarence, (brother of Edward IV and Richard III), b. 1449, d. 1477 (murdered).

Anne, b. about 1454, m. 2ndly, 1472, d. 1485 (m. 1st, 1470, Edward, Prince of Wales, son of King Henry VI).

Richard III, 'King of England and France and Lord of Ireland' 1483, b. 1452, d. 1483 (killed).

19

RICARDVS · III · ANG · REX ·

King Richard III second husband of Anne Neville whom she married after the death of the Prince of Wales in 1471.

Warwick Castle, birthplace of Anne and her sister Isabel.

Tewkesbury and the death of the Prince of Wales, when Anne was a ward of the Duke of Clarence, Richard Duke of Gloucester wanted to marry her. Clarence was opposed, because as the husband of her elder sister Isabel, he hoped to claim the entire Warwick fortune for himself. To keep Anne away from Richard, Clarence disguised her as a kitchen maid. Richard recognized her while she was serving a meal, and took her to the sanctuary of St. Martin's le Grand. In 1472 or thereabouts Richard bullied her until she agreed to be his wife. This is absurd. Royal dukes were not served by lowly kitchen maids, but by members of the nobility. Richard would never have seen Anne under such circumstances.

The Modern Interpretation

By ignoring the Tudor chroniclers and passing judgement after using earlier documents, historians have concluded that Richard was probably Anne's first love. Before meeting Edward Prince of Wales, Anne had led a sheltered life at Middleham as the daughter of a wealthy and ambitious man. While her father Warwick the Kingmaker was promoting the Yorkist cause, Anne had been taught to hate the Lancastrians, including Edward Prince of Wales. Then her father changed sides and went off to France to intrigue with Queen Margaret for the restoration of Henry VI.

To Anne's consternation, in 1470 she was abruptly ordered to France to wed the Prince of Wales, and she was probably bewildered by her father's change of direction. She had never met this future husband but she did know Richard of Gloucester. When he was twelve and she eight, Richard had come to Middleham as a knight apprentice, and had stayed two years with the Neville family. The fact that he was fit to be a knight belies the description of him as a deformed hunchback.

After the death of the Prince of Wales, the Duke of Clarence, Anne's brother-in-law, made her virtually a prisoner to keep her away from Richard. When Richard found her posing as a kitchen maid, Anne, not Clarence, was responsible for the ruse. A plausible explanation was that Anne had run away from the Duke of Clarence's house, adopted the disguise herself and found employment elsewhere. Then she contrived to send a message to Richard and he took her to the sanctuary of St. Martin's le Grand to keep her safe from Clarence until he could make arrangements for the marriage they both wanted.

As Duke and Duchess of Gloucester, Richard and Anne made their home at Middleham Castle in Yorkshire. The location suited Richard, for like Anne's late father he was a Warden of the West Marches, responsible for keeping the peace along the border. His duties took him from home frequently to deal with

21

raids into the north of England by the Scots. At Middleham in 1476, Anne and Richard's only child was born, a son they named Edward. Like her mother, who had borne only two children, Anne was not strong. Nor was the little Edward a sturdy child. Yet, during Anne's lifetime there was no conclusive evidence that Richard wanted to get rid of her so that he could marry a woman who would give him more children.

In April 1483 King Edward VI died. The Duke of Clarence was also dead, and Richard was the only surviving brother. Under the terms of the King's will, Richard was to be the guardian of his children. Leaving Anne to make a more leisurely journey to London with their son, Richard hurried there. He was concerned that the Queen's Woodville relatives would take charge of his nephews, the new King Edward V and Richard Duke of York, and seize the regency. Richard knew that Edward IV had made him guardian to curb the ambitions of the Woodvilles.

Once in London, Richard removed the twelve-year-old King and his nine-year-old brother from their mother's custody and lodged them in the royal apartments in the Tower. Next he went ahead with plans for the young King's coronation, set for 22 June 1483, amidst doubts about the wisdom of permitting an under-aged monarch to reign. The minority of Richard II had been a time of instability, while that of Henry VI had been more disastrous. Richard tried to sense the mood of the English people and concluded that they would welcome a mature man on the throne.

On 9 June he called a meeting of the council. The Dowager Queen Elizabeth was a member, but he excluded her. To the council he queried whether the Queen's marriage with his brother had been legal. She had been married before and the proper dispensations had not been obtained. The council deliberated and decided that the late King's children were illegitimate. By an Act of Parliament the heirs of Edward IV were disinherited. Richard Duke of Gloucester, the next in line, was proclaimed King.

There is no doubt that Richard did usurp the throne, but from his point of view he did so in the best interests of the country. He was unjust in setting aside his brother's children's inheritance, but he was not ruthless enough afterwards in eliminating other claimants to the throne. (If Richard had had his nephews murdered in the Tower, why did he leave so many other potential heirs alive?)

Anne was now the Queen. Her son was the new Prince of Wales. Anne was in no condition to enjoy her new role and elevated status. The Warwick seed was not strong. Her sister Isabel had died of what was apparently consumption, leaving two children, Edward Earl of Warwick, and Margaret (who would

become the loyal friend of the third Princess of Wales). By the time Anne was Queen she, too, was showing symptoms of consumption. Richard was aware of Anne's condition and knew that she had not long to live. It seems unlikely that he would try to have her poisoned, as the Tudor chroniclers state; he had only to wait for her natural death. His son was also frail, but Richard hoped that young Edward would outgrow his frailness. Richard himself had been a delicate child yet he had overcome his sickliness as he grew older.

Anne began her journey to London in easy stages, accompanied by her son, and they joined Richard in time for the coronation at Westminster Abbey on 6 July 1483. Afterwards Richard set off on a royal progress to show himself to his new subjects. Anne and Edward joined him at Warwick Castle and accompanied him to York. There, in solemn procession, Edward beside them, Richard and Anne walked through the streets. At York on 8 September Richard staged the investiture of their son Edward as Prince of Wales. Afterwards Anne and Edward returned to Middleham Castle.

Richard's hopes that Edward would grow up to be a strong man were soon ended. The boy died at Middleham on 9 April 1484 in his eighth year. Anne, gravely ill, passed away at Middleham on 16 March 1485, and did not live to share her husband's downfall.

By the time Anne died, opposition to Richard's rule was growing. It centred on Henry Tudor, the son of Margaret Beaufort, Countess of Richmond. Henry's father was Edmund Tudor, the illegitimate son of Owen Tudor and Katherine, the widow of Henry V, which made his claim to the throne tenuous. On his mother's side, too, Henry Tudor's claim was through illegitimate lines. Margaret Beaufort was descended from John of Gaunt and his third wife Katherine Swynford. All the Beaufort children were born before their parents' marriage, and while they were declared legitimate afterwards, such a decision was easy to overturn.

Evidence uncovered in pre-Tudor sources does not suggest that the deposed Edward V and his brother Richard Duke of York were dead when King Richard III set off with his army to confront the forces of Henry Tudor on the field of Bosworth, in Leicestershire. On 22 August 1485, Richard was killed and Henry emerged victorious, seizing the throne as Henry VII.

Historians are now inclined to conclude that three well-known myths about Richard III, based on Tudor chronicles, are ill-founded. First, Richard did not have his nephews murdered, for he had no more to fear from them once they had been ruled illegitimate than from other claimants to the throne that he did not try to eliminate. Henry VII, however, did, and the princes were murdered, not during Richard's brief reign, but in the early stages of Henry's.

Second, Richard did not coerce Anne Neville into marrying him; theirs was a love match. Her earlier marriage to Edward Prince of Wales had been forced on her. Third, there was no evidence that Richard considered poisoning Anne in order to marry Edward IV's daughter Elizabeth, his nephews' sister. A Pope might countenance a marriage between first cousins, but never between a man and his own niece. Besides, if her brothers were illegitimate, so was she, and any heirs that resulted from such a union would be open to challenges by other claimants to the throne.

Richard III was probably not the monster of Tudor fiction, and Anne Neville probably found in him a caring husband. The tragedy of Anne's life was that she was the pawn of Warwick the Kingmaker, of

Richard's that he lacked the ruthless streak that might have led him to eliminate Henry Tudor before he could be overthrown by him. The Tudors made no such mistake. Among Henry's early acts was the imprisonment of Anne's nephew, Edward Earl of Warwick, her sister Isabel's son, in the Tower. Later Edward was beheaded. Likewise John, an illegitimate son of Richard III, was killed. In the reign of Henry VIII, Margaret, Edward of Warwick's sister and Anne's niece, was also beheaded.

Hidden by Tudor chroniclers was the story of the love of a young girl for an apprentice knight that blossomed as they grew older. Thwarted by the ambitions of Warwick the Kingmaker, it was retrieved by the couple themselves. Anne's life ended before her thirtieth birthday. By dying before the Battle of Bosworth she was spared the abuses she certainly would have suffered at the hands of Henry Tudor.

Anne was raised at Middleham Castle, Yorkshire and lived there again as Queen. Ruins of the castle in the mid-18th Century.

24

Katharine of Aragon
1485 – 1536

The third Princess of Wales was Katharine, a daughter of Ferdinand King of Aragon and his wife Isabella, in her own right Queen of Castile. The marriage of Katharine's parents joined their two kingdoms, uniting much of what is now modern Spain. Katharine's tragic story is better known than are the lives of her two predecessors. Katharine was the first wife of Henry VIII, and her failure to give him a healthy son led to his protracted battle to have their marriage annulled. However, Katharine's earlier marriage to Henry's elder brother, Arthur, had made her a Princess of Wales.

Katharine, the youngest of five children, was born in the palace of the Archbishop of Toledo on 15 or 16 December 1485, (the year that Anne Neville, the second Princess of Wales died). At that time Spain had no capital, and the seat of government was wherever the King and Queen were residing. The rulers moved about because the royal household was large and soon exhausted the nearby food resources.

When Katharine was only three years old, a delegation arrived from England and arranged her betrothal to two-year-old Arthur, Prince of Wales and heir to Henry VII. Ferdinand and Isabella pledged a dowry of 200,000 crowns, half to be paid at the time of the marriage, the remainder two years later. In England the legal age for a marriage was twelve years for a girl, fourteen for a boy. Thus the marriage could

not take place until after September 1500, Arthur's fourteenth birthday. Ferdinand and Isabella were glad of the waiting period, to see whether Henry VII would be deposed by some other claimant to the throne. The execution in 1499 of Richard III's nephew, Edward Earl of Warwick, was ordered by Henry VII to reassure Katharine's parents that his throne was secure.

Katharine was raised to be a devout Catholic in the Spanish mould, and she was never able, in her later life, to tolerate bending the rules. Her firm religious convictions were a source of great strength in the future, and the cause of her greatest suffering.

She was short, with auburn-gold hair more reminiscent of the Plantagenets than of the Spanish people, with good reason. Her mother Isabella was a great granddaughter of John of Gaunt, whose second wife was a Princess of Castile. Katharine chose as her personal badge the pomegranate, the emblem of Granada, which her parents captured from the Moors in the interval between her betrothal and her departure from Spain. She suffered from frequent colds and fevers, ailments which the English climate could hardly be expected to alleviate. But as the year 1501 opened, the time of embarkation was at hand.

In advance a proxy marriage was performed. After delays caused by rough seas, she landed at Plymouth on 2 October 1501. Characteristically her first act after setting foot on English soil was a visit to

Henry VIII as a young man.

Ludlow Castle in Shropshire, where Katharine lived as Princess of Wales, is now a ruin.

where Philip died and was succeeded by their son Charles.

Again Katharine was in the King's good graces and lived at court. Prince Henry, a tall, strong youth seemed happy about marrying Katharine. Still Ferdinand and Henry VII haggled over the dowry, a matter ended only when King Henry was dying. He ordered Henry to marry Katharine, before he passed away on 21 April 1509. The wedding took place on 23 June at the church of the Observant Friars, near Greenwich. Thus ended a seven year ordeal in England for the Spanish Princess. The coronation was set for 29 June.

The streets were decorated with tapestries and cloth of gold. Henry rode forth in a crimson velvet robe trimmed with ermine, followed by lords temporal and spiritual. Katharine rode in a litter carried by two palfreys, in a gown of white satin richly embroidered, a circlet of jewels in her hair, followed by the kind of retinue she knew was her right. The new emblem of the monarchy was the rose of the Tudors and the pomegranate of Spain, symbols used on livery and on banners at jousts and tournaments. The marriage began well. Although Katharine was twenty-three and Henry not quite eighteen, he was proud of his Queen and devoted to her.

The royal treasury was in a healthy state for Henry VII had been acquisitive and thrifty. Ferdinand, who no longer had an excuse for withholding the rest of the dowry, sent the other 100,000 crowns. At last the future looked rosy for the foreign Princess. The devotion of the English people was as strong as ever, although the court was divided. Some courtiers favoured an alliance with France; others supported Katharine's more powerful nephew Charles.

For a better balance of power, Henry VIII decided to have his sister Mary, aged eighteen, marry King Louis XII of France. Louis lived only three months after the wedding. Mary became the Dowager Queen of France, and Henry sent Charles Brandon Duke of Suffolk to bring her home. The Duke married Mary in secret before leaving France. Katharine liked the match because it made Mary happy.

Meanwhile Katharine was trying her best to provide Henry with a healthy male heir. From the time of her marriage in 1509 until 1518, she was pregnant at least seven times. The first child, who arrived in May 1510, was stillborn. A son Henry was born on New Year's Day 1512 and immediately created Prince of Wales. Two months later he died. Three other stillborn children were boys. The only child who thrived was Princess Mary, born on 18 February 1516. Henry was delighted, but still anxious for a son. No woman had ever been Queen of all England in her own right, and he feared that his people might not accept Mary.

Then, to Katharine's discomfiture, one of her

maids, Elizabeth Blount, gave birth to Henry's natural son in June 1519. Henry acknowledged the child and named him Henry Fitzroy. Now the King felt that Katharine was to blame for their lack of living children, since he had performed well with Elizabeth Blount. Nevertheless, at that stage in their marriage Henry was still devoted to Katharine although they quarrelled because she was upset over the existence of Henry Fitzroy.

The English people remained happy with their Queen. In 1517 that love was reinforced by her stance during a revolt of the apprentices. The revolt was suppressed, and hundreds of boys were sentenced to be executed. Katharine knelt before Henry and begged him to spare the boys' lives. Henry relented, and her action further endeared her to the masses.

By 1519 the three most powerful rulers in Europe were Henry VIII of England, Francis I of France, and Charles V of Spain. Charles' prestige was enhanced when he was elected Holy Roman Emperor on 28 June. Courtiers assumed that Katharine favoured Spain and Charles, but she held a broader view, the unity of all Christendom against the Turks and their leader "Solyman the Infidel". Henry and Francis organized a spectacle to take place the following year, a meeting of the French and English courts near Calais, which England still possessed. And in May 1520, Charles came to England and met with Katharine in Canterbury, the first time they had seen each other.

Charles departed on 31 May, and that same day Henry and Katharine set off to meet Francis of France, accompanied by courtiers, soldiers and horses. Henry's retinue comprised 3,997 people and 2,087 horses, while in Katharine's were 1,175 people and 775 horses. A new town was built at Guisnes for all these visitors. Francis, his Queen Claude and court, were housed in equal splendour at nearby Ardres. The meeting of the two kings took place in what was called "The Field of Cloth of Gold" after the extravagance of the displays put on by each side.

Over the next few years, Henry's affection for Katharine cooled somewhat. She was upset when the King bestowed many titles on young Henry Fitzroy, his bastard son, and gave him his own household. To Katharine, the King's behavior suggested that he hoped to find a way to secure the succession for this boy, disinheriting Princess Mary. With worry her bouts of illness and fevers returned, and she frequently had an upset stomach. Pregnancies were now beyond her capabilities, and she knew that she could never give Henry the son he so desperately wanted. Yet she was his lawful wife in the eyes of God, and there was nothing that could be done to change that.

In August 1525, when Princess Mary was nine years old, Henry decided she should have her own household. Her residences included Ludlow Castle, Tickenhill, Thornbury and Beaulieu. Mary's governess was Margaret Pole, Countess of Salisbury, who had befriended Katharine twenty-four years before. Katharine assumed that Mary would one day rule, as had Isabella of Castile, and she arranged for the Humanist scholar, Dr. Richard Fetherston, to become Mary's tutor. Also, Mary's training as a devout Catholic was continued. Although separated, mother and daughter kept in touch regularly by letter. Two years later Katharine first learned that Henry wanted to leave her.

Henry began, on 17 May 1727, by arranging to have himself summoned to a secret court at York House, the palace of Cardinal Wolsey. There the Archbishop of Canterbury and Wolsey charged him with living in sin with his brother's widow. On 22 June, Henry went to see Katharine, told her that his conscience was bothering him and they must part. Katharine was horrified. If Henry was right, her soul was in danger and Mary was illegitimate. Yet she was not entirely taken by surprise. Rumours had been flying about on what the public called the "King's Great Matter".

The remaining nine years that Katharine was to live were a battle on her part to remain the Queen and to protect Princess Mary's right to inherit the throne. She stoutly maintained that her marriage to Arthur had been in name only, and was never consummated. Agreeing to an annullment would be tantamount to admitting that she had had sexual relations with Arthur and had sinned in marrying Henry. If she accepted Henry's offers of the allowance permitted a Dowager Princess of Wales, then she would be sinning. The pattern was set even before Henry fell in love with Anne Boleyn and resolved to be free to make her his Queen.

Henry held most of the trump cards, and he had the power that made the outcome inevitable. He had, however, to be discreet in his harrassment of Katharine, for he dared not offend the public. Had Katharine borne him healthy sons, the marriage would have endured, although the King probably would have taken mistresses from time to time as Katharine aged. Because all her sons had died, Henry began to wonder if God were punishing him, and to question the status of the marriage as well as to look for the means to end it. The Queen, firm in her position, appealed to the Pope, and to her nephew Charles, as Holy Roman Emperor, to support her. A frustrated Henry then sought to break her will. Most of her friends deserted her out of fear of the King, who forced Margaret Pole, Countess of Salisbury, to leave Katharine's service. In an attempt to bully Katharine into agreeing to be the

Dowager Princess of Wales, Henry stopped all communication with Princess Mary.

In January 1531, Henry ordered Katharine to leave Windsor and accept a house at Ampthill, in Bedfordshire. In December 1532, Anne Boleyn was pregnant, and he could not dally long if this child were to be legitimate. In January 1533, after annulling his first marriage himself, Henry and Anne were married. That April a delegation from Henry visited Katharine at Ampthill and asked her to renounce her title as Queen and agree to be known as the Dowager Princess of Wales once more. She refused. That summer Katharine's now much reduced household was moved to Buckden, on the edge of the fen country, and placed in the Bishop of Lincoln's palace. Buckden was a damp place, quite unsuitable for one who suffered from frequent colds and fevers as Katharine did.

Now Henry's wrath was directed at his daughter Mary, then living at Beaulieu. Anne Boleyn's child was born on 7 September 1533, a girl the King named Elizabeth, bitterly disappointed she was not a son. At the age of three months Elizabeth was given her own household at Hatfield. Soon Mary's household was dispersed, her staff dismissed, and she was sent to live in the home of her tiny half-sister.

Margaret Pole, Katharine's faithful friend, offered to serve Mary without pay, but Henry refused the offer. Mary's sole attendant was a chambermaid whom she suspected of spying on her. Small Elizabeth's household was run by Lady Shelton, an aunt of Anne Boleyn, who was Mary's governess with orders to treat her harshly and as a servant. Mary was often slapped by Lady Shelton, and her confessor was sent away and replaced by a Lutheran of Anne Boleyn's choosing. All this was done to break her spirit. If Katharine could not be conquered, perhaps the daughter was not as strong-willed. Perhaps, too, Katharine would give in if she knew what Mary was suffering.

In the spring of 1534 Katharine was moved from Buckden deeper into the fen country to Kimbolton Castle, where she was virtually a prisoner, allowed to see few people. Her health deteriorated, amidst rumours that she was being poisoned. Her sole comfort was her faith, her conviction that it was better to suffer than to yield to Henry's wishes and their implications for Mary's legitimacy.

In December 1535 Katharine became gravely ill. She rallied for a time, but now thin and wasted she lingered until 7 January 1536. The Bishop of Llandaff, Jorge de Atheque, himself Spanish and now her confessor, annointed her and read her a last service. She asked God to forgive Henry and died at two o'clock that afternoon. Henry ordered her buried in the Benedictine abbey church of Peterborough with the honours due a Dowager Princess of Wales. Mary was not allowed to go to the funeral nor did Henry attend. The banners that flew over Katharine's grave displayed the pomegranate badge, the arms of Charles V Holy Roman Emperor and Prince Arthur, but not those of Henry VIII.

Throughout her life in England, Katharine was a kindly person, concerned for the well-being of the poor, and after her marriage to Henry VIII an obedient wife, as she had been trained to be in Spain. She refused to bow to Henry in only one matter of importance, the status of her marriage. She lived and died a martyr to her beliefs. Yet Katharine shared the best years of Henry VIII's life. He became something of a buffoon as, through five additional marriages he sought more heirs. His three surviving children all reigned. Edward VI, his son by his third wife, died of tuberculosis at age sixteen. Mary succeeded him and England paid a sad price for the terror and rejection she had endured as a girl. Elizabeth, the unwanted daughter of the ill-fated Anne Boleyn, reigned so successfully that she gave her name to one of the greatest ages in England's history.

"I beseech you . . . let me have justice and right!" Katharine makes a personal appeal to Henry VIII at her trial before leaving the court and refusing to return.

32

Caroline of Ansbach

1683 – 1737

The fourth Princess of Wales was Caroline, a daughter of John Frederick the Margrave of Brandenburg – Ansbach, and Eleanora of Saxe-Eisenach. She was the consort of George Augustus (later George II), the heir to the Elector of Hanover who, in 1714, became George I of Great Britain. Caroline was the first Princess of Wales who received her title at the same time as her husband was created Prince of Wales. When George I became King, George Augustus and Caroline had been married for some years.

Caroline was born in 1683 at Ansbach. When she was four years old her father died. In 1696 her mother followed, leaving her an orphan at age thirteen. Her guardians were King Frederick I of Prussia and his Queen, Sophia Charlotte, a sister of George Augustus' father, the future George I.

Caroline grew to be a big woman, a blond "Nordic" type who would have looked well in a Wagnerian opera. She enjoyed her life in Berlin, the most important court in Germany, and she acquired a reputation as a bluestocking. She read widely and had an excellent memory. While not an intellectual, she was happiest in the company of successful writers of the day.

Caroline's pleasant life in Berlin ended in 1704 with the death of the King of Prussia when she was twenty-one, and she returned home to Ansbach. By that time George Augustus, also born in 1683, was the Electoral Prince of Hanover. He had heard that Caroline was an interesting woman, and he made a visit to Ansbach, supposedly incognito, in June 1705. No one was fooled, least of all Caroline, but she found her suitor attractive and a betrothal was concluded.

George Augustus was third in line of succession to Queen Anne of Great Britain, who had borne seventeen children, none of whom had lived. Ahead of George Augustus were his grandmother, the Electress Sophia of Hanover, and his father George. Their claim rested on the Electress Sophia's mother, Elizabeth Stuart, a daughter of King James I. Britain had turned to Hanover to find a successor to Queen Anne because the son of the deposed James II, was a Catholic and barred from the succession.

Caroline was a good choice for George Augustus. His early life had been wretchedly unhappy. His parents, George of Hanover and Sophia Dorothea of Celle, had two children. When George Augustus was eleven and his sister, also Sophia Dorothea, nine, their father accused their mother of adultery and had her imprisoned in the Castle of Ahlden. (There she remained until her death thirty-two years later.) Her two children were placed in the custody of their grandmother, the Electress Sophia. George Augustus adored his mother, and he hated his father for the way he treated her.

George Augustus grew to be a dapper, small man with bright blue eyes. His portraits, made when he was middle-aged, do not suggest this. He grew portly as years passed. He was not intelligent, but fascinated by soldiering, which led him to accumulate an impressive knowledge of military history and tactics. In 1708 he was allowed to have a command, and under the Duke of Marlborough he served with distinction at Oudenarde.

The married life of George Augustus and Caroline divides into three periods. Prior to the death of Queen Anne, they were the Electoral Prince and Princess of Hanover. From 1714 to 1727 they were Prince and Princess of Wales. After George I died they were King and Queen of Great Britain, for in 1707 Scotland had been united with England and Wales.

George Augustus and Caroline were married on 2 September 1705. At first their home was at Kalenburg, the capital of Hanover. The royal family home was Herrenhausen Palace, two miles away, surrounded by formal gardens and forests. In January 1707, Caroline gave birth to their first son Frederick Louis. For reasons never made clear, neither of his parents loved Frederick. He was small and dark with sallow skin and did not resemble them, but no one suggested he was not their son. His parents' dislike of him echoed the unhappy relationship that existed between George Augustus and his own father.

Soon after Frederick's birth, Caroline contracted smallpox, but she recovered and was not disfigured. While still in Hanover, she gave birth to three daughters — Anne, later the Princess Royal, in November 1709; Amelia Sophia in June 1711; and Caroline Elizabeth in June 1713. Their mother was easy-going, tolerant and able to adjust to any situation. The court at Hanover was dull, but she accepted her surroundings and made the best of them. George Augustus was a ladies' man, who could not help falling in love regularly and the first person with whom he wanted to share his joy was his wife. Caroline took these amours in stride, confident that he would always come back. Her one inexplicable trait was her dislike of her first-born, Frederick.

Early in 1714 the Electress Sophia died, making Caroline's father-in-law first in line to the British throne. Then on 1 August 1714, Queen Anne died, and George was King. At once he set out for England with George Augustus, leaving Caroline to follow with the children. Caroline, now Princess of Wales, set out from Hanover with servants and nursemaids, and the three little Princesses. Frederick, not yet eight years old, was left behind in Hanover, to be brought up by tutors, deprived of his immediate family.

Caroline reached London on 15 October and the coronation was staged on the twentieth. The smoldering resentment which George Augustus felt for his father, which was returned in kind, now broke into

wholesale war. The King was not popular, for the image of a monarch whose wife was a prisoner in Hanover, accompanied by two plump mistresses, who had not bothered to learn English, was not an appealing one. The mistresses were soon nicknamed Elephant and Castle in scurrilous pamphlets so popular in England.

The behavior of the Prince and Princess of Wales was in striking contrast. Both had learned some English, although George Augustus was more fluent in French. Immediately the Waleses were better liked than the King. George I's court consisted of Germans he had brought with him; Caroline and George Augustus chose English courtiers. Two courts evolved, the old one of the King, the young one of the Waleses, and George I quickly became jealous of his son and daughter-in-law.

The following year, 1715, when the Jacobites rose on behalf of James Stuart (the son of the deposed James II) and proclaimed him King in Scotland, George Augustus begged the King for a command, and was refused. Denied worthwhile work, George Augustus helped Caroline enliven their own court. Both became interested in the arts. George Augustus liked the works of Handel, while Caroline enjoyed the company of writers. She held morning drawingrooms that were a great success. Gradually politicians who opposed the government were drawn to the young court. The young couple badly wanted a home of their own, away from St. James' Palace, and in 1716 they seized their opportunity.

The King went on a visit to Hanover, and the Waleses moved with their children to Hampton Court. Caroline was pregnant, and when on 28 October her labour pains began, she was being attended by a British doctor. A German doctor arrived from St. James', asserting that the King had ordered him to attend the royal family. While they quarrelled over which should look after the Princess of Wales, she gave birth to a stillborn son, her fifth child. By implication the King was to blame for the loss of her baby.

On 2 November 1718, Caroline again gave birth, to a son named George William. By that time the conflict between the King and George Augustus had reached new extremes of bitterness. The King thought of having the Prince of Wales killed. In Hanover such a murder would have been a simple matter, England, however, was a constitutional monarchy, not an absolute one, and the sovereign could be held accountable if he broke the law. Bearing in mind that the Britons had once, through that unfortunate tool, Parliament, beheaded an annointed King, and sent the man who might now be reigning as James III into exile, George was cautious. He contented himself with forbidding George Augustus to use any royal

34

residence. Caroline could stay because the birth of Prince George William was so recent, as would the other children.

Caroline refused, even though the King would not let any of the children leave, and she departed with her husband. They took a house in Leicester fields, which stood on what is now the north side of Leicester Square, and she resumed her morning draw-ingrooms. The Leicester House set was launched, and the King felt helpless. He could not even have the satisfaction of cutting George Augustus off without a penny, for Parliament voted the Prince his income.

Caroline and George Augustus now tried to bring their neglected son Frederick over from Hanover, but the King would not give his consent. One heir in the country was causing enough trouble and he did not want two.

Towards the end of January 1718 the baby, Prince George William, became ill. The King had him moved to Kensington Palace so that Caroline could visit him without causing friction. On 6 February 1718, the baby died and Caroline returned to Leicester House, determined to regain custody of her three daughters from the King.

That summer George Augustus leased Rich-mond Lodge, in Richmond Old Park, as a summer

The old castle at Ansbach where Caroline was born.

Sir Robert Walpole, 1st Earl of Orford, by the studio of Van Loo 1740. Walpole and Caroline led the Leicester house set and the Prince of Wales followed.

Contemporary cartoonist's view of Caroline's adored younger son William Augustus, Duke of Cumberland.

George, Prince of Wales, husband of Caroline and later King George II. A portrait by Kneller.

residence. The young court was gaier than ever. With the Prince of Wales' sponsorship horse races were organized, and house parties when the men went stag hunting. Caroline revelled in the company of opposition politicians and literary figures. Her Ladies in Waiting were often George Augustus' mistresses, which suited her, for she could keep an eye on them. For herself she preferred the society of clever men, but just as friends.

One of Caroline's cronies was Robert Walpole, a leader among opposition Members of Parliament. He was not an official leader, for there was no official opposition. Britain was a one-party state dominated by Whigs. Tory members were few in number, usually country gentlemen. The government consisted of Whigs who agreed with the King, and Whigs who disagreed with him formed the opposition (which might be numerically in the majority). Walpole and Caroline spent much time together, but there was no physical attraction. She was stately and rather handsome; he was corpulent and ugly. Their minds were where they met.

Both were rather earthy, power-hungry, and pragmatic. They let George Augustus think himself the leader of the Leicester House set. Both were successful in feeding him ideas that he felt were his own. The Waleses spent the summer at Richmond Lodge, the winter at Leicester House. Politicians with ambitions cultivated them. The King was ageing and the new order would be directed by George Augustus, backed by the popular Caroline.

As the year 1720 opened, the King's ministers were concerned over the split in the royal family's ranks, and at the way the opposition gathered around Leicester House. There were still many Jacobites in the land, and if the Hanoverian monarchy faltered, there might be strident demands for the restoration of the Stuarts. A reconciliation would also bring some useful members of the opposition to the side of the King.

The matter required negotiations. The Prince did not want to return to any royal residence, nor did Caroline, but both wanted custody of their three daughters. A compromise involving the politicians was reached. If Walpole, and Charles Viscount Townshend, a statesman of wide experience, would join the government, the Prince and Princess of Wales could remain at Leicester House and the King would give back their children.

Before these negotiations were completed, Anne the Princess Royal contracted smallpox in April 1720. Very alarmed, Caroline begged the King to permit her to be with her child, now ten years old. Before the King made up his mind, Princess Caroline Elizabeth, nearly seven, also succumbed. The King allowed Car-

The Music Party. This famous picture painted about 1733 shows Frederick, Prince of Wales, the neglected eldest son of Caroline, making music with his sisters (from left) the *Princesses Anne, Elizabeth and Amelia who had been taught by Handel.*

oline to go to them, but she was not to bring her own doctor nor any medicines. Caroline accepted his terms and hurried to St. James' Palace. Fortunately the girls recovered, and soon afterwards all three Princesses moved to Leicester House.

The girls were not very strong, and they suffered from frequent colds and bronchitis. In April 1721, Caroline gave birth to her seventh child, William Augustus, a sturdy boy who thrived. (While still in his twenties he commanded his father's army. As Duke of Cumberland he is remembered as the Butcher of Culloden, when, in 1746 he brought the Jacobites' efforts to restore the House of Stuart to a close). William Augustus was followed by a daughter, Mary, in February 1723. Caroline's last and ninth child was another

daughter, Louisa, born in December 1724, when she was thirty-nine years old. This last birth was difficult and Caroline suffered an umbilical rupture.

The old and young courts existed in a state of armed truce. George Augustus was biding his time, for the King was now sixty-four and might not last much longer. Many of the Prince and Princess of Wales' opposition friends had gone over to the government's side, and politics was less exciting at Leicester House. Caroline's drawingrooms continued, attended by, among other writers, Alexander Pope and Jonathan Swift — wits who enjoyed satirizing the government. In 1727, Walpole, now Sir Robert, was the King's chief minister. Swift, whose *Gulliver's Travels* was published that year, was a favourite of Caroline although her mind was no match for his.

Life was not as gay at Leicester House, for George Augustus was being careful not to irritate the King and his ministers. The Prince still liked Walpole, and he did not want to alienate him by a too-spirited leading of the opposition. Behind him, of course, was Caroline, who missed Walpole and intended to renew the friendship once George I was out of the way.

The King was thinking of a suitable bride for Frederick, now nineteen, and suggested Frederick's cousin Princess Wilhelmina of Prussia. Her mother was George Augustus' sister Sophia Dorothea, but her brother disapproved. George Augustus was fond of his sister but thought her husband King Frederick William quite mad.

In November 1726, George Augustus' long-suffering mother, Sophia Dorothea, died in her prison at the Castle of Ahlden, mourned mainly by her son who had not seen her in thirty-two years. The following May, leaving George Augustus as Regent, the King, now sixty-seven, set out for a holiday in Hanover. He got only as far as Osnabruck, where he died on 11 June 1727.

The Prince and Princess of Wales were at Richmond Lodge when the news reached London. Sir Robert Walpole came himself to inform them that they were now King George II and Queen Caroline. At the coronation, Caroline wore borrowed jewels, because George I had given Queen Anne's gems to his mistresses. The ceremony over, George II appointed Caroline his Regent and went off to Hanover to claim his mother's belongings. On his return he hung two portraits of her in places of honour in St. James' Palace.

As King, George II became decidedly dull. Except for Caroline's activities, his court was no longer gay. He was growing portly, and becoming nostalgic about things German. Now that his parents were both dead, he made more visits to Hanover, taking an interest in the affairs of his other domain. As at Leicester House, Caroline remained the power behind the throne. Politicians wanting action would take their ideas to Walpole. He would discuss them with Caroline, who in turn would convince George II that the ideas originated with him. George probably knew that he was being manipulated, and he was given to bullying Caroline in public, well aware that he was the inadequate one.

The public was not ignorant of the true situation either, for this jingle was in circulation:

"You may strut, dapper George, but 'twill all be in vain, We know 'tis Queen Caroline, not you, that reign".

Early in 1728, the King and Queen received alarming news from Hanover. The neglected Prince Frederick, now twenty-one, had tried to elope with his cousin, Princess Wilhelmina of Prussia. George II ordered Frederick to come to England. Frederick arrived in the autumn, and the King created him Prince of Wales. For a time Caroline got along fairly well with Frederick, but George II resented his presence from the start. On the other hand, Prince William Augustus Duke of Cumberland, seven years old when Frederick rejoined the family, was the favourite. Gradually Caroline sided with George II in hating the heir, and said she wished Frederick were dead so that William Augustus could inherit the crown.

In the spring of 1735, leaving Caroline as Regent, George II returned to Hanover. He fell passionately in love and shared his good fortune with Caroline, in letters over thirty pages long. The Queen was not flustered. George belonged to her and could not manage without her. The following year, when Prince Frederick married, Caroline advised her daughter-in-law to be tolerant, as she had always been.

The umbilical rupture Caroline had suffered at the time of the birth of Princess Louisa in 1724 was to prove fatal to her. The only person who knew about it was the King. Both felt that an ailment in such a private place was not something to be shown to a doctor. On 9 November 1737, Caroline developed frightful pains in her abdomen with severe vomiting. Her physicians bled her and gave her various potions, which did nothing to relieve her suffering. Finally on 11 November, a very worried King told the doctors about the rupture.

She lived nine more days during which the doctors lanced the protruberence, now gangrenous, and tried to cut away the mortified flesh. As she lay dying, George II was distraught. To comfort him, Caroline told him he must marry again.

"No. No," he wept. "I'll have mistresses".

He meant what he said. Although he lived another twenty-three years and had mistresses, he never did remarry after her passing on 20 November 1737.

As George II's life was nearing its end, he made a will specifying that his coffin was to have a side removed, as was Caroline's, so that their ashes would mix forever. Both were laid to rest in the Henry VII chapel of Westminster Abbey, the last King and Queen to be buried there.

Caroline's first-born, Frederick, was Prince of Wales (but never King) and his wife was the fifth Princess of Wales. Of her other surviving children, Anne married William the Prince of Orange and ruler of the Netherlands, Amelia and Caroline Elizabeth remained single, as did William Augustus Duke of Cumberland. Mary married Frederick of Hesse-Cassel, and Louisa married Frederick V of Denmark.

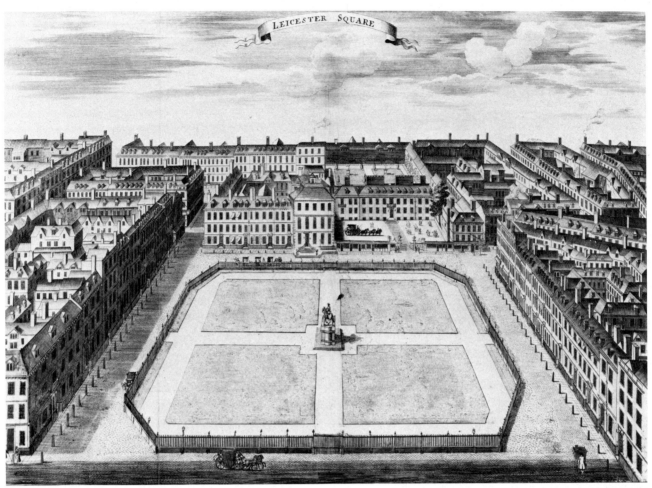

Leicester Square, London with Leicester House centre right where two successive Princesses of Wales held court.

Augusta of Saxe-Gotha

1719 – 1772

The fifth Princess of Wales, Augusta of Saxe-Gotha, was the consort of Frederick Prince of Wales, the unloved son of George II and Caroline of Ansbach. Augusta's parents were Frederick II Duke of Saxe-Gotha and Magdalene Auguste of Anhalt-Zerbst. She has the doubtful distinction of being the only Princess of Wales who did not hold the love of the people throughout her life.

George II picked Augusta as a suitable bride for his son while on a visit to Hanover in 1736. On his return to London the King informed Prince Frederick that his bride had been chosen. Before acquiescing, the Prince of Wales sent a spy to Saxe-Gotha. When the spy reported that Augusta was not unattractive, and neither deformed nor insane, Frederick informed the King that she was acceptable.

Augusta arrived at Greenwich on 25 April 1736, knowing a little French but not a word of English. Her mother thought that after twenty years of Hanoverian rule, everyone in England would be speaking German. She was tall, pleasant-looking although her face was pitted by smallpox scars, friendly and not overly intelligent. Two days later Augusta and Frederick were married in the chapel of St. James' Palace. The bride was seventeen years old, the groom twenty-nine. In order to demonstrate that the marriage would be consummated, the couple underwent the humiliation of being bedded together and having courtiers troop past, and one remarked that the Prince's nightcap was rather taller than a grenadier's hat.

Frederick was disliked by both the King and Queen. When George I became King, Frederick's parents, then the Prince and Princess of Wales, took up residence in England. They left Frederick with tutors in Hanover and he did not come to England until he was twenty-one. While others thought him charming and intelligent, the King described him as a "half-witted coxcomb", while the Queen was convinced he was impotent. Of the wedding night, she noted that Augusta looked exhausted after the ceremony, but so refreshed the following morning that consummation had not been part of their activities after the nuptial bedding.

In choosing Augusta of Saxe-Gotha, the King and Frederick had compromised. While Frederick had once tried to elope with a Prussian princess, he had also refused his father's first choice, Princess Charlotte Aurelia of Denmark, when he discovered that she was deformed and retarded.

Frederick's own first choice was Lady Diana Spencer, a granddaughter of the first Duke and Duchess of Marlborough. Frederick and the Duchess made a plan for the wedding to take place at her lodge in Windsor Great Park, but the King's first minister, Sir Robert Walpole, objected. An alliance with any of the great English families might offend other such families. A German princess, with no connections in the country, would be politically preferable.

Lady Diana Spencer's nephew, John, was the first Earl Spencer, from whom the present Princess of Wales is descended; her father is the 8th Earl Spencer. Like his father and the present Prince of Wales, Frederick was musical. Written records state that he played the viola, but a portrait of Frederick with his three eldest sisters shows him playing what is certainly a cello.

Following their wedding, Augusta and Frederick stayed at St. James' Palace, but soon moved to Hampton Court with the rest of the royal family. By the end of the year there were rumours that Augusta was pregnant. As the time for the birth of her child drew near, Frederick became determined that it should not be born at Hampton Court with his mother as a suspicious witness. He apparently had difficulty making arrangements to remove his wife, for he did not procure a coach until 31 July 1737, when, with Augusta he set out for St. James' Palace. Poor Augusta was already in labour, but Frederick, very agitated, ignored her pleas to stop so that she could be delivered in comfort. They reached St. James' just before the baby, a girl they named Augusta, actually arrived.

Queen Caroline was furious. She wanted to be present to make certain the child really was Augusta's. Only two Lords of the Council arrived in time to witness the birth, and the baby was described as a "little rat of a girl about the bigness of a large toothpick case". On seeing her, the Queen agreed that the child was Frederick's, as she was a "poor, little, ugly she-mouse". (That same she-mouse would thrive and become the mother of the sixth Princess of Wales). Augusta was spared further derogatory remarks on the part of her mother-in-law, for Queen Caroline died in November 1737.

Refusing to live in any of the royal residences, Frederick rented a house in St. James' Square from the Duke of Norfolk. There the future George III was born on 4 June 1738. Frederick and Augusta soon took up residence in Leicester House, acquiring a summer house at Kew. As in his father's day, Leicester House attracted the opposition, and there existed old and young courts. This time, however, Frederick was the leader in fact as well as name. Unlike Caroline, Augusta took no part in politics and concentrated on her children.

The younger royals were a contented family. Frederick was a good husband and father, although he took Augusta to fortune tellers and went himself in disguise to bull baitings. At home, Frederick and Augusta arranged amateur theatricals, which Frederick thought would give their son George confidence in public speaking, and were closer to their children than

George II and Caroline had been to theirs. Born to Augusta at Leicester House were Edward Augustus (Duke of York) in 1739; Elizabeth Caroline in 1740; William Henry (Duke of Gloucester) in 1743; Henry Frederick (Duke of Cumberland after the death of his uncle, William Augustus) in 1745; Louisa Anne in 1749; and Frederick William in 1750.

In 1745, Prince Charles Edward Stuart landed in the Scottish Highlands and raised a Jacobite army to restore his family to the throne. Frederick asked for a command, but as with his father in 1715, the King would not allow the heir to serve. The favourite younger son, William Augustus Duke of Cumberland, received the command of the army that defeated the Jacobites.

In March 1751, the family was staying at Kew. Augusta was pregnant with their ninth child. On the fifth, Frederick caught a cold that turned to pleurisy and by the twentieth he was dead.

After the funeral, Prince George, twelve years old and the new Prince of Wales, was sent to live with the King at Hampton Court, while Augusta was allowed to keep Leicester House and Kew and remain in charge of her other children. The young Prince did not stay long with his grandfather. The boy was backward for his age, and the King was short on patience. Somewhat disgusted with this heir, the King sent him back to Augusta. On 11 July 1751, Augusta gave birth to a daughter, Caroline Matilda, at Kew.

Now the Dowager Princess of Wales, Augusta had to look beyond her hitherto small domestic world in the interests of safeguarding her children's rights. She felt threatened by her brother-in-law, the Duke of Cumberland, who might persuade the King to place him ahead of Frederick's children in the succession because they were minors. Fortunately the King was fond of Augusta, and when he wanted to visit Hanover he chose her as Regent over the Duke of Cumberland. George II settled 50,000 pounds on Augusta, which, added to her revenue as Dowager Princess of Wales, gave her an income of 64,000 pounds. She needed it for she contributed to many charities, and Frederick had left substantial debts.

She found that she had to involve herself in politics, and she saw every development in terms of how it might affect her children. After Frederick's death there were three factions. One was the King's. Second, and the least important because of his unpopularity was the Duke of Cumberland's. The third was Augusta's at Leicester House. She took as her chief adviser John Stuart, 3rd Earl of Bute, a friend of Frederick, whom he had made Lord of the Bedchamber the year before his death. Bute was a Scot who had sat in the House of Lords in the 1730s.

Frederick, Prince of Wales by Mercier.

Picture from The Gentleman's Magazine *marking Frederick's death in 1751.*

Hampton Court Palace. Augusta lived here after her marriage to the Prince of Wales. Frederick however was deter- *mined that their first child should not be born under the same roof as his mother Queen Caroline.*

Although he had no sympathy with the Jacobites, the fact that he was a Scot made him distrusted by certain politicians and the public. But Augusta grew to depend on him, and they became friendly with the upcoming leader in opposition, William Pitt.

The education of her children, especially the two older Princes, required her attention. With Bute's help, she selected two new tutors. To his credit, the boys developed well after he helped supervise their education, but he had fixed ideas that influenced the Prince of Wales and caused trouble in his later reign. Because the King's ministers knew of Bute's hold over both Augusta and the Prince of Wales, he was unpopular with the government.

In 1756 the Prince of Wales turned eighteen, and now, if the King died there would not be a Regency. The King suggested that the Prince have his own household. Young George wanted to appoint Lord Bute his Groom of the Stole, but the King disapproved. The Prince refused to accept a household unless Bute got the appointment and the King at last agreed. Bute was then able to push William Pitt's career in government. Pitt eventually became the leader of the government during the Seven Years' War with France, advocating new, successful policies.

Of more concern to Augusta was a marriage for the Prince of Wales. The King, still the Elector of Hanover, favoured Princess Caroline of Brunswick, as a way of protecting Hanover from Prussia. Princess Caroline's mother was a sister of Frederick II (the Great) of Prussia, and such an alliance would prevent Frederick attacking the Electorate. Augusta, who disliked all Prussians and the Duchess of Brunswick in particular, did not approve of the King's choice. The Prince of Wales himself declared that he was an Englishman, and he did not want a German Princess at all. Personally, Augusta thought that the young Prince was too immature to take on the responsibility of a wife and family.

At that stage the Prince was more interested in getting a command, now that Britain was at war. Edward, his younger brother, was allowed to serve in the navy as a volunteer, but the King, following traditional Hanoverian policy, did not want the heir involved. The Prince made do by falling in love with Lady Sarah Lennox, a daughter of the Duke of Richmond. Pitt was as upset over the Prince's desire to marry into one of Britain's great families as Walpole had been when Frederick Prince of Wales had been set on marrying Lady Diana Spencer. Pitt advised the Prince to accept a German princess who would be neutral. Augusta was probably relieved that her eldest son was being kept out of both the war and marriage.

44

Augusta's elder sons George, Prince of Wales and Edward,
Duke of York with their tutor the Reverend Francis Ayscough.

The Dowager Princess of Wales soon suffered the first devastating blow since the death of her husband. On 4 September 1759 her fourth child, Princess Elizabeth Caroline, died before her nineteenth birthday. Now Augusta had even more cause to value Lord Bute's friendship, for he helped her accept this loss. At the same time, Augusta and Bute were trying to revitalize the Leicester House set, in their opinion for the good of the country, which they felt was endangered by the war. The King was now the remarkable age of seventy-six, and could not last much longer. Guided by Bute, Augusta was looking for a change in direction for the future King George III.

Bute had definite ideas about how the country should be run that he had instilled into both Augusta and young George. It should be governed by the King personally, not by his ministers. They had become too powerful during the reigns of George I and II. The First spoke no English, and the Second was too preoccupied with the security of Hanover in his later years. Bute wanted to prepare for the reign of George III by making certain that his first government would have in it men who were of like mind, who were willing to let the power acquired by the ministers revert to the King.

On 25 October 1760 King George II died, and during the period of mourning news arrived from America that General Jeffrey Amherst had captured Montreal, the last holdout by the French in Canada. Pitt's policies had succeeded, and there remained only some way to end the war in Europe and the West Indies. The new King George III was at Kew when he was informed of his grandfather's death, and he hurried to London. Because of Lord Bute's efforts Leicester House had gained some supporters, and his protégée the new King was more self-assured.

George III (and Hanover's new Elector) was now twenty-two years old. He lacked any sense of political know-how, and was an uncomplicated person, upright, abstemious, the picture of respectability and decorum – the work of his mother Augusta. ''George'', she is supposed to have told him often. ''Be a King''. Judging by the conduct of her younger sons, she succeeded only with the eldest in instilling a high moral tone. Edward Duke of York, William Duke of Gloucester, and Henry Duke of Cumberland were all rather wild. As his wife the King agreed to accept Princess Charlotte of Mecklenburg-Strelitz. Their engagement was announced on 8 July 1761. George III's coronation, delayed so that his bride could participate with him, took place on 22 September.

Leicester House now became the old court over which the Dowager Princess of Wales presided, the ever more unpopular Lord Bute as a substitute-consort. The young court was that of the King and Queen. For a change, too, the young court was the dull one, the old generating the excitement, of the wrong sort. While Lord Bute tried to keep a foot in each camp, advising both the King and his mother, gossips whispered that he was Augusta's lover. Outside Parliament, in the press the politicians and journalists were waging war on Bute.

In November 1762 a preliminary treaty of peace was signed with France, and George III took great pride in ending the Seven Years' War. Augusta is said to have observed "Now my son *is* King of England". The London street mobs might have agreed with her, but as the cessation of hostilities was being proclaimed, Lord Bute was assaulted by a gang of demonstrators and had to be rescued by soldiers. Worse was to come. By the time the final peace treaty was signed, George III had become unpopular over the way, trained by Bute, he was trying to rule without his ministers. Journalists castigated the King's "Scotch favourite", and openly accused Augusta of having him as her lover. Political cartoonists symbolized John, Lord Bute with a jack boot, the Dowager Princess by a petticoat.

Finally Bute had the good sense to offer to retire. The King was appalled, but Bute was adamant, and George III accepted his resignation on 8 April 1763. Nevertheless parading and burning a jack boot and a petticoat remained a popular sport. Accepting a lover was totally out of character for Augusta. She was deeply religious, of Calvinistic background, and she lived by the moral code she tried to instill in her children.

In 1765 George III fell ill with what was probably porphyria, the disease believed to have caused his mental illness in later life. From January to March he had several attacks at Buckingham House, the residence where he and Queen Charlotte lived. A Regency Council was appointed and the King excluded Augusta's name on the advice of his ministers. In May, Parliament passed the Regency Act, by which time the King had relented and added his mother's name to the list for the Council. His ministers changed their minds when they found that the Members of Parliament did not want the nation to think they had had a hand in humiliating the Dowager Princess of Wales. Horace Walpole, Sir Robert's son and a Member, commented "Obnoxious as the Princess was, the heinousness of the insult to her, and the treachery of the King shocked all mankind".

Augusta had yet another matter that preoccupied her. Her eighth child, fifteen-year-old Prince Frederick William, died on 29 December 1765. Again Lord Bute consoled her. Although Bute no longer had any political influence, the public continued to believe that he was Augusta's lover. He had a house at Kew not far from hers, which fuelled the rumours.

The following year, in September, Edward Augustus Duke of York, then aged twenty-eight, died unmarried while visiting Monaco. Again Augusta needed Lord Bute to console her, which probably helped keep alive the story of their supposed illicit relationship. In May 1768 a mob paraded a jack boot and a petticoat on a gibbet through Cornhill. This was cruelty in the extreme, for on the thirteenth, at age nineteen, Augusta's seventh child, Louisa Anne, died. Four of her nine children had now passed away.

Although both Augusta and Bute were virtually retired, Jack Boot and Petticoat remained in the public mind the symbols of their purported influence over the King. A new political journalist's letters were appearing in newspapers under the pseudonym "Junius", letters more vicious than most. Late in 1771 "Junius" declared, "it would indeed be happy for this country" if the Dowager Princess of Wales should die. In fact she was dying, probably of cancer. Some who knew her said that she would die in her coach for she wanted to "take the air" every day. The end came on 8 February 1772 when she was fifty-two years old. The public was delighted; she was mourned only by her immediate family.

She died intestate, an indication of how naive she was, leaving only 7,500 pounds, which fuelled rumours that she had given large sums to Lord Bute. Donations to charities that depended on her and the settling of Frederick's debts were the real reason why her estate was so small.

Of the five children who outlived her, Augusta, the eldest, married Charles William Duke of Brunswick, despite her mother's dislike of that family. George III was a devoted, if dull, husband to Queen Charlotte and a somewhat pig-headed King, and ten of their children were born before the Dowager Princess of Wales died. In September 1766 William Henry Duke of Gloucester secretly married Maria the Dowager Countess of Waldegrave, a natural daughter of Sir Edward Walpole (Sir Robert's son), and did not tell the King until after Augusta's death. Henry Duke of Cumberland's marriage to a widow, Lady Anne Horton in 1771, was only slightly more acceptable.

Caroline Matilda, born after her father Frederick's death, fared the worst of all. In 1765 she married the unstable Christian VII of Denmark, when she was fourteen years old and an unwilling bride. Joshua Reynolds, who painted her pre-nuptial portrait, admitted that he could not do her justice for she had been weeping so much. In Copenhagen she bore the King one child, and then took as her lover his Chief Minister, the German doctor Count Johann vol Struensee. In a coup d'état in 1772, she was imprisoned in

Elsinore Castle. George III secured her release by sending a squadron of the Royal Navy towards Denmark. She was allowed to go to Hanover, where she lodged in the Castle of Celle, but she had to leave her child behind in Denmark. She died in Celle in 1775, possibly of the porphyria thought to have afflicted George III during his reign.

Augusta of Saxe-Gotha, Princess of Wales throughout her adult life and never Queen, had a public image she did not deserve. Her dependence on Lord Bute made her distrusted by the press and the public. Her inability or unwillingness to end that relationship brought about her own fall from the public's favour and no doubt hastened her death.

John Stuart, 3rd Earl of Bute. Sir Joshua Reynolds' painting shows this confidant of Augusta and chief Minister of George III wearing the robes of the Garter.

Three satirical attacks on Bute's relationship with the Royal Family. Top: Augusta and her son flank Bute in a suggested design for a new coin. Centre: Medal struck to mark the election of John Wilkes as Lord Mayor of London, 1774. Bottom: The Boot (Bute) falls from power.

Caroline of Brunswick
1768 – 1821

The sixth Princess of Wales was Caroline, a daughter of Charles William Duke of Brunswick and Princess Augusta of Great Britain, the elder sister of George III. Caroline was the only Princess of Wales whose husband and cousin, the future George IV, never loved her at all. Had she lived in these times she would have been a feminist. She objected to the double standard whereby her husband could have mistresses while she was expected to remain chaste. Her outlook got her into trouble, but she never lost the affection of the British public.

Caroline was born on 17 May 1768, six years after her Prince of Wales, into a court that was the gayest in Germany. She was fond of children, friendly, a warm person with a ready laugh, no inhibitions and appallingly frank. In 1793, while with his regiment in Germany, Prince Frederick Duke of York visited Brunswick and afterwards he informed his father George III that Princess Caroline would make a fine consort for his brother the heir to the throne. At that time the Prince of Wales had no intention of marrying for the sake of the succession. Fredcrick, respectably married to Frederica the Princess Royal of Prussia, could produce the needed heirs.

By 1794 the situation had changed. Frederica Duchess of York could not have children, and the Prince of Wales was deeply in debt and in need of extra sources of revenue.

For years he had been devoted to Lady Maria Fitzherbert, a Catholic, and was supposed to have gone through a Catholic marriage ceremony with her in secret. He was also enamoured of Frances Countess of Jersey, a friend of his mother, Queen Charlotte. He lived lavishly and his debts amounted to more than a quarter of a million pounds. If he married someone acceptable, Parliament might be persuaded to increase his allowance, enabling him to pay some of his creditors. He was not much interested in who that woman would be and he took his younger brother's recommendation at face value. In November 1794 he sent Sir James Harris, Earl of Malmesbury, to Brunswick to arrange the marriage and bring Caroline to England.

Malmesbury obeyed, although he suspected the marriage would fail. Caroline, then twenty-six, was stocky with a short neck, dowdy, rough-spoken, and unwashed; her redeeming feature was a fine head of golden hair. Privately he thought the Prince of Wales would be revolted by her, but his orders were to escort her to England, not to give an opinion on her suitability. On longer acquaintance her good qualities emerged. She had a fine sense of humour although she lacked tact and good sense.

Others who had reservations about the match were Queen Charlotte, who disliked the House of Brunswick, and the bride's father. The Duke of Brunswick had heard of the Prince of Wales' penchant for mistresses, which he knew Caroline would find hard to tolerate. He warned his daughter that she must take no notice, to which she retorted that if the Prince could have lovers so could she. She was shocked when the Duke informed her that a Princess of Wales who took lovers could be charged with high treason.

Caroline and Malmesbury left Brunswick on 30 December 1794. En route Malmesbury advised Caroline that the Prince of Wales was fastidious and washed daily, always changing his linen. He suggested to one of Caroline's ladies that the Princess should accustom herself to bathing often and wearing clean underclothing and stockings. Caroline found this novel advice, but with a laugh agreed to follow it.

They landed at Gravesend on 5 April 1795, and proceeded to Greenwich where, to Caroline's disgust, they were met by Lady Jersey, her newly appointed Lady of the Bedchamber. Before she left Brunswick her mother had warned her of Lady Jersey's relationship with the Prince of Wales, but Caroline could not follow her father's council to be tolerant. Furthermore, Lady Jersey persuaded her to change to a dress of which she knew the Prince would never approve, and suggested more generous use of rouge, although Caroline's own natural colour was strong. The change had the desired effect. When Caroline first met the Prince at St. James' Palace, she prostrated herself before him, which gratified the King but not his son. The Prince drew her to her feet and turned to Malmesbury.

"Harris", he said. "I am not well. Pray get me a glass of brandy".

Caroline, too, was unimpressed. After the Prince had gone she told Malmesbury, "I find him very stout and by no means as handsome as his portrait".

Nonetheless they were married on 8 April 1795, in the Chapel Royal at St. James' Palace, and the bridegroom was drunk. Among Caroline's attendants was Lady Charlotte Spencer, a daughter of George John 2nd Earl Spencer, later a Home Secretary. The newly-weds lived at Carlton House, Pall Mall, and managed to stay together until 7 January 1796, when Caroline gave birth to their only child, Princess Charlotte.

By the spring, after many fights, they were maintaining two separate households under the same roof. The Prince was asking the King for a separation, while Caroline was complaining to him about having Lady Jersey in her service. Despite all the advice given her, Caroline never hesitated to speak her mind, often in front of journalists, who relished her candour. The Prince of Wales, with his extravagant habits and loose morals, was unpopular with the press and the common people.

In June 1796 the Prince let Caroline leave Carlton House and set up her own establishment. For the next two years she rented the Old Rectory at Charlton on the Thames, but she kept a set of rooms at Carlton House for visits to Princess Charlotte. In 1798 George III appointed Caroline a Ranger of Greenwich Park, which increased her income. She moved to the larger Montague House, Blackheath. Apart from frequent visits to her daughter, whom she adored, she stayed at Blackheath, where she filled in her days playing the harp, painting and studying English.

She contributed to charities, and adopted some orphans found around the dockyards. She entertained her neighbours and naval officers, and in fact had her own small court — boisterous and indiscreet. Montague House also attracted the Prince of Wales' political enemies. During the reign of George III, England ceased to be a one-party state wherein Whigs opposed Whigs. The Tories were an influential party, usually favoured by the monarch and his heir. Gossips suggested Caroline was up to no good, although her amusements were innocent. She played chess with Lord Minto, and talked gardening with Walter Scott, a rising novelist. Both Minto and Scott thought her disconcertingly flirtatious. Caroline did enjoy male company and was a tease. She saw no reason why estrangement from the Prince of Wales should imply living in seclusion.

The King was on Caroline's side. Often, when Princess Charlotte was visiting Montague House, he joined them. If that rather sober monarch found Caroline acceptable, were the reports on her vulgarity exaggerated? The Prince, however, resented his father's friendship with Caroline, and sought to prove her unfit to raise Princess Charlotte.

By 1804 Caroline and the Prince were battling over the education of Charlotte, now eight years old, and over who should have custody of her. She received her own household at Warwick House, a rather gloomy edifice near Carlton House, where her governess was Martha, Countess of Elgin. The Prince of Wales wanted Charlotte's visits to Montague House strictly supervised by Lady Elgin because of Caroline's notorious behavior. The Prince insisted that Caroline visit Charlotte as a guest, and not remain long.

While these arrangements were being hammered out, a neighbour of Caroline's near Montague House, Lady Charlotte Douglas, told an extraordinary story. She was a frequent visitor of Caroline. In 1802 Caroline told her she was pregnant, and had covered her tracks by spending a few nights at Carlton House so that the Prince could not claim that the child was not his. The child in question was a boy named William Austin, who, Caroline later publicly claimed, she had adopted.

In 1805 the Prince demanded an enquiry, and by the summer of 1806 the King ordered a commission to investigate the conduct of the Princess of Wales. Called the "Delicate Investigation", the commissioners interviewed Lady Charlotte Douglas and many of Caroline's servants. According to Lady Charlotte, she was herself pregnant when she visited Caroline in 1802. Caroline confessed herself in like condition, and also offered, when the time of Lady Charlotte's "accouchement" drew near, to bring a bottle of port and a tambourine to entertain her while she was in labour. A servant then testified that Rear Admiral Sir Sidney Smith had once been found in Caroline's room in an indecent condition.

Other servants testified that George Canning (later the Foreign Secretary) and the artist Thomas Lawrence, who had painted Caroline's portrait, had been intimate with her. Then two doctors who attended Caroline in 1802 testified that she had not been pregnant. Apparently she had cooked up the story to shock Lady Charlotte Douglas. The commissioners found Caroline not guilty of adultery but rash. The boy William Austin, whom Caroline nicknamed Willikin, remained at Montague House, a substitute for Princess Charlotte, to whom Caroline had very little access.

For some time after the "Delicate Investigation" Caroline was not received at court by the King. As time passed he forgave her and allowed her rooms in Kensington Palace. This happy situation ended in 1811 when the King's illness that had plagued him for many years came to a head. The Prince of Wales was named Regent, and Caroline found herself out in the cold, forbidden to see Princess Charlotte. Since she could no longer use Kensington Palace, she took a house in Connaught Place. There her mother, Augusta Duchess of Brunswick, now a widow, joined her.

The Prince Regent was finding his daughter a handful. Charlotte seemed too much a hoyden, high-spirited and gauche, in fact her mother's daughter. Caroline badly missed Charlotte and she wrote abusive letters to the Prince Regent demanding the right to visit her. In 1812 when Charlotte turned sixteen, the Prince Regent decided that a husband would calm her down and the search for someone suitable began.

When on 23 March 1813 the Dowager Duchess of Brunswick died, Charlotte was permitted to spend two hours at Connaught Place with Caroline. About the same time a sympathetic Parliament voted Caroline an income of 50,000 pounds. She suggested the amount be reduced to 35,000 pounds. Widely reported in the press, this gesture contrasted sharply

When Caroline and the Prince of Wales separated soon after their marriage, Caroline went to live at Montague House, Blackheath.

With Bartolomeo Pergami on her right, and riding on an ass, the Princess of Wales enters Jerusalem in the summer of 1816.

Acclaimed by the populace, Caroline now Queen goes to the House of Lords in August 1820 to be tried.

Miniature of King George IV as Prince of Wales by Richard Cosway.

Princess Charlotte of Wales, Caroline's daughter, and her husband Prince Leopold of Saxe-Coburg at the opera.

with the Prince Regent's continued extravagances and endeared Caroline to the public.

By July 1814 Caroline, who no longer had her mother for company and rarely saw her daughter, decided to travel on the continent for a while. On the twelfth, Princess Charlotte slipped down a backstairs in Warwick House and arrived very distraught at Caroline's house in Connaught Place. Charlotte informed her mother that the Prince Regent had arranged her betrothal to William IV Prince of Orange, a man she detested. Caroline comforted her and sent for her Whig champion in the House of Commons, Henry Brougham. He counselled Charlotte to return to Warwick House and to effect a reconciliation with her father.

Tearfully Charlotte agreed. The Regent assured her she need not marry the Prince of Orange, for his ministers disapproved of the match. Early in August with Willikin, Caroline boarded the frigate *Jason* for her voyage to the Elbe River and Brunswick. Caroline entered into her travels with zest. Reports of her exploits shocked her daughter, and the Privy Council advised the Regent not to allow her to return to England. Charlotte, too, made disclosures about Montague House on certain of her visits that reflected badly on her mother. On one occasion Caroline had put her in a bedroom with a captain of dragoons, and locked the door on them.

Abroad Caroline continued on her merry way, taking a villa on Lake Como, squired by the attentive Bartolomeo Pergami, an Italian and a veteran of Napoleon's Russian campaign. In 1816, with Pergami she toured the Greek Islands, visited Constantinople, Jericho and Jerusalem. There she made a grand entrance with twenty-five attendants and what was described as 200 "opportunists". She instituted the Order of St. Caroline, making Pergami her Grand Master.

Back in London the Regent allowed Princess Charlotte to marry the man of her choice, Prince Leopold of Saxe-Cobourg, who agreed to reside in England. (Later Leopold was elected King of the Belgians, and he was Queen Victoria's beloved uncle.) The marriage of Leopold and Charlotte took place on 2 May 1816, and they made their home at Clarmont, Surrey. On 27 October 1817, Charlotte died giving birth to a stillborn son. Now there was no immediate heir to the throne, and the Regent's younger brothers abandoned their mistresses and bastard children to marry and beget some. Caroline remained on the continent with Pergami; there was nothing to entice her back to England.

In 1818, hoping to obtain grounds for a divorce, the Regent appointed a three-man Commission to go to Italy and determine whether Caroline's relations with Pergami were adulterous. The government advised against divorce. The situation was complex, for Pergami was not a British subject and could only be prosecuted if he came to England. The Regent let the matter drop, more concerned that his mother, Queen Charlotte, had died on 17 November 1818.

On 29 January 1820, George III died, and the Regent was proclaimed King George IV on the thirty-first. Whether the King and his ministers approved or not, Caroline was now Queen consort. The government had doubts about how courts in the countries she visited would receive her. Having the Queen travelling about the continent with the man everyone thought was her Italian lover posed a diplomatic dilemma. At home, George IV decreed that the Queen should be excluded when prayers for the royal family were offered in the churches, and he implored his ministers to arrange a divorce, but they again counselled no such move. George IV's Tory ministry was unpopular, and the Whigs were on Caroline's side.

The Tories' hope of keeping Caroline abroad was soon dashed. As soon as the winter was over she set out for England to claim her rights. With Willikin, now eighteen, she crossed the Channel to Dover on 5 June, where crowds welcomed her enthusiastically. As she drove through London in her landau more crowds cheered; sentries in front of Carlton House presented arms. She shouted "Long live the King" as she rode along Pall Mall. At the time she was doing the monarch a great service. The common folk were battling for political power and social justice, and riots frequently broke out. Seeing the Queen made people set aside their own woes. They regarded the courageous Caroline as much a victim of the King and his ministers as they were themselves.

The King was still determined not to have Caroline as his consort. The government prepared a Bill of Pains and Penalties, to deprive Caroline of her title as Queen and have her marriage declared null and void without offering the proof of adultery that would be required in a court of law. Hearings which the Duke of Wellington described as unpleasant were held in an annex off the House of Lords, which Caroline could attend although she was not permitted to give evidence. Caroline stayed at Brandenburg House, in Hammersmith, and was cheered as her carriage passed through the streets. The King remained at Windsor awaiting the outcome at a safe distance. The evidence against Caroline was circumstantial, but on 6 November 1821, a vote was taken in the House of Lords which passed by a narrow margin. It was never sent to the House of Commons, where it certainly would have been defeated by the Members. They knew how the public felt about Caroline, and would hold up to ridicule the King's infidelities. The Queen had won; the masses rejoiced.

On 29 November a service of thanksgiving was held in St. Paul's Cathedral. Caroline drove there in state, and while her name was never mentioned, she was allowed to occupy the bishop's throne.

The coronation was set for 19 July 1821. Caroline sent a message from Brandenburg House enquiring what ladies would be in her train and what she should wear. When the King replied that she would have no part in the ceremony and must not attend, she was furious. On the day she drove to Westminster Abbey, but was refused admittance. George IV had scored a triumph of sorts, but Caroline was still his Queen even though he had prevented her being annointed with him.

Later in July 1821 he set out on a state visit to Ireland, the first ruling monarch to go there who was not at the head of an army. On the thirtieth, while attending a performance at Drury Lane Theatre, Caroline was seized by severe abdominal pain and taken back to Brandenburg House. A message was dispatched to the King, who stopped at Anglesey. Proceeding would be unpopular if the Queen were on her deathbed. Caroline lingered until 7 August, and the King respected her wishes to be buried in Brunswick and to have on her coffin the inscription: "Caroline of Brunswick, the injured Queen of England".

The King ordered that her body be taken down the Thames on a state barge and put on a man-of-war bound for the Elbe River, to avoid a procession through the streets of London and possible public demonstrations. As the Admiralty did not have a suitable barge handy, the authorities decided to move her coffin overland to Harwick, where a vessel was waiting and to avoid taking it near central London.

The people refused to be foiled. A mob forced the small procession to turn down Tottenham Court Road and follow the streets to Temple Bar. In the disturbances one man was killed. The King's enemies of course blamed him for the disorder. George IV left Holyhead on 12 August, but once in Ireland he delayed for five days of "mourning" before he entered Dublin. When he did he wore a black armband. Caroline would have been the first to laugh at this outward symbol of the grief George did not feel.

The masses were probably right in their enthusiasm for Caroline of Brunswick. She arrived in England, a little vulgar but willing to learn and adapt. When faced with little but complete rejection on the part of her husband, she resolved to live her own life. When her husband would not keep her company, she went in search of men who would, and provided gossips with endless sources of surprise and dismay.

Of the two children Caroline loved, her only daughter predeceased her. Willikin, who travelled

with her on the continent, died in a lunatic asylum in Chelsea in 1849.

Mark's satire on the Prince and Princess of Wales' matrimonial predicament.

Death of Caroline

Alexandra of Denmark
1844 – 1924

On 23 November 1918, the Dowager Queen Alexandra was travelling with Queen Mary in an open landau, preceded by King George on horseback, enroute to a victory celebration at Hyde Park. The excited crowd surged round the royal family and even attempted to climb onto the carriage. A mounted officer moved so close to offer protection that his horses's head lay in Queen Alexandra's lap. The Queen calmed the nervous horse by stroking its nose and bowed to the admiring crowd with complete composure.

Over fifty-five years before, on 7 March 1863, Princess Alexandra of Denmark arrived in England for her marriage to the Prince of Wales (later Edward VII) and rode in an open carriage through London with the Prince and her parents Prince and Princess Christian of Denmark. Then too an excited crowd surged round the carriage, some even attempting to kiss her hand and a nervous horse of the escort began to kick. Its hoof caught in the rear wheel of the carriage but before a serious accident occurred, the Princess calmly reached out and released the animal.

A world had changed in the half-century that had passed but the character of Alexandra had not, nor had the love of the people for her. Born Alexandra Caroline Marie Charlotte Louise Julia in Copenhagen on 1 December 1844, "Alix" was the eldest daughter and second child of Prince Christian of Schleswig-Holstein-Sonderburg-Glücksburg, heir to the Danish throne, and Princess Louise of Hesse-Cassel. When Alexandra married Edward of Saxe-Cobourg-Gotha, the Prince of Wales and son of Queen Victoria, she became the seventh Princess of Wales and the first in forty-three years. It was a title she was to hold for nearly thirty-eight years, longer than any other princess before or since.

To say that Alexandra took England by storm when she arrived for her wedding would be an understatement. The reaction was comparable to that when Lady Diana Spencer emerged on the royal scene in 1981. From Alix's arrival at Gravesend, through her triumphal procession into London, to her arrival at Windsor, the people fell instantly in love with the shy nineteen-year-old. After all they had not witnessed a marriage of a Prince of Wales for sixty-eight years and to get a bride so beautiful was a bonus. One burly countryman pronounced "I have come all the way from Carlisle to see her, and I would stand here in the rain till this time tomorrow if I could only set eyes on that bonny face again". In Hyde Park the newly created Volunteers were situated along the route to present arms. Their enthusiasm got the better of their marshal spirit and they "gave the salute at command, and then, forgetting all discipline, broke their ranks and ran after the carriage".

The wedding itself was held in St. George's

Gûle Palais, the modest home in Copenhagen where Princess Alexandra lived as a girl.

Alexandra riding a camel in Egypt 1868. She greatly regretted not being able to travel to India and not seeing the Empire but she took part in many Empire celebrations in Britain.

Chapel, Windsor Castle and was a private ceremony, not the public royal wedding of today. But celebrations were held in towns and villages throughout Britain and the Empire. Queen Victoria was still in official mourning for Prince Albert who had died fifteen months before, so she watched the ceremony from a private balcony pew. The wedding gifts were later put on display at South Kensington Museum and the crowds that queued to see them were immense.

Alexandra's was an arranged marriage but it was not without genuine love and affection as is sometimes believed. Queen Victoria and Prince Albert had decided that "Bertie" needed to settle down with a good wife as his wayward tendencies were already evident by 1859. Following his hugely successful tour in Canada in 1860 the planning began in earnest. Princess Alexandra of Denmark was not considered suitable because of her relatively modest background (her father was poor and not of the senior branch of the Danish royal family, though chosen to succeed the childless king) but primarily because Victoria did not wish a Danish connection as Denmark was hostile to Prussia. Finally the Danish royal family had an unsavoury reputation. There was no fault with Alexandra or her parents but Victoria was obsessed by "wicked uncles" and Alexandra had many in that category.

Victoria hoped for a German princess but she knew that none of the eligible ones were attractive enough to suit Bertie's tastes. When her daughter Vicky, Crown Princess of Prussia recommended Alexandra in spite of Prussian-Danish hostility, the Queen and Prince Consort agreed that Bertie and Alix should meet and an "accidental" encounter was arranged in Speyer. On seeing Alix's picture Albert remarked "from the photograph I would marry her at once". Victoria noted "The Photograph of Princess Alexandra is indeed lovely, what a pity she is who she is!" Bertie was attracted to Alix and she to him but Bertie was more in love, or perhaps infatuated, with an actress, Nellie Clifden, his first liaison and was uncertain about embarking upon marriage.

Both families were upset by Bertie's hesitation, and when the Prince Consort learned the cause he was greatly shaken and died after becoming ill while visiting his son to settle the matter. Though the cause was typhoid fever he had contracted at Windsor Castle, Victoria blamed Bertie for his death and began to doubt the wisdom of the marriage for Alexandra's sake, "for were the poor girl to be very unhappy I could not answer for it before God had she been entrapped into it". But Bertie too had been shaken by his father's death and he determined to marry Alexandra and be a good husband. When the Queen travelled to Denmark to observe her future daughter-in-law she was immediately entranced by Alix's beauty and character. "How He would have doted on her and loved her!" the Queen wrote, thinking of Prince Albert. The affection between Victoria and Alexandra was mutual and grew, although the years ahead often saw many disagreements, criticisms and jealousies on Victoria's part. The Queen truly thought of her as another daughter and "a real blessing to me". On 9 September Bertie proposed to Alix at Laeken in Belgium through an opportunity arranged by Victoria's uncle, King Leopold of the Belgians.

Alexandra's upbringing had been happy and affectionate but strict and frugal. The Gûle Palais (Yellow Palace) in Copenhagen, next to the royal Amalienborg, was a palace in name only. Not being wealthy, Alix was not pampered by luxury and often mended her own clothes. Her great loves were music and dancing, gymnastics, riding and animals and her mother had taught her the importance of proper bearing. She was noted for the sweetness of her character though she had little conception of time and punctuality and could be selfish as well as kind. Her physical beauty was marred only by a scar on her neck which led her to devise a jewelled "dog-collar" to cover it, thus creating a piece of fashion that has lasted till today. She had also inherited from her mother ostosclerosis – a form of deafness that can be brought on or accentuated by illness or pregnancy and which was to torment her later in her life.

Alexandra's initial popularity in Britain did not wane. If anything it matured into a genuine popular affection for her as a person. The public charities she immediately gave her attention to were those concerned with children, inaugurating the Orphan Asylum at Slough and the Home for Little Boys at Farningham that summer. She also became a fashion setter – her hair style of two ringlets at the side soon being adopted by other young ladies.

The young royals were the catalyst for the release of pent-up enthusiasm among younger society and Marlborough House, the Prince and Princess' London home, became the centre of social activities with the Princess even more popular than the Prince. On the Queen's birthday the following year the Prince reviewed a regiment of Volunteers of which he was colonel-in-chief. As they marched past, the officers directed their looks and thus inadvertently their salutes to the Princess instead of the Prince.

Alexandra's kindness, often becoming sentimentality, was ever present and endeared her to all she met. While on a tour of Egypt in 1868-69 she brought back a Nubian orphan, Ali Achmet, to Sandringham where he was baptised and raised. She also brought back a black ram that was fated to be slaughtered but had wisely taken a liking to her. Alexandra was undoubtedly the greatest collector of animals in the royal family. In addition to horses, dogs and cats, she acquired flying foxes, goats, parrots, rabbits, cockatoos, donkeys, bears and tigers in considerable quantities and kept them, bears and tigers included, at Sandringham.

Sandringham, the Norfolk house bought for Bertie by Prince Albert was Alexandra's real love. For though she enjoyed society as much as her husband, she was essentially a domestic person. After their initial bliss, Bertie's affections wandered again and Alexandra learned to live with his infidelity, reputedly saying once "after all, he loved me the best". This was apparently true, for while Bertie was incapable of being faithful to one woman he was at the same time devoted to Alexandra. Alexandra herself never even considered being unfaithful though she had many platonic admirers.

Following complications at the birth of Princess Louise in 1867 her deafness became progressively worse and she also developed rheumatism which left her with a permanent limp. In fact there was fear for her life at the time. Though she overcame the limp with a gliding movement that was then adopted by society ladies, the two afflictions made it difficult for her to enjoy the company of her husband's circle and she withdrew more into her domestic life though never abandoning her society position.

Alexandra's sentimentality, warmth and selfishness were most evident with regard to her children. There were six, beginning with Prince Albert Victor ("Eddy"), born 8 January 1864, Prince George, 3 June 1865, Princess Louise, 20 February 1867, Princess Victoria, 6 July 1868, Princess Maud, 26 November 1869, and Prince John, 6 April 1871, who lived but a day. Her letters to Prince George (later King George V) from his childhood to mature adulthood were addressed and signed by both parties as "Mother-dear" and "Georgie" and quite without any selfconsciousness on George's part. Alexandra's problem with her children was that she could not quite accept that they would grow up, perhaps from the not unnatural but selfish desire not to lose them. Princess Victoria, who never married, suffered the most from this as Alexandra grew to depend on her and probably did not wish to see her married. Alexandra could also be embarrassingly kind to her nieces and nephews to whom she sent children's toys when they were adults.

Alexandra's great disappointment as Princess of Wales was in not being allowed to accompany the Prince on his 1875 trip to India. She had developed a fascination and interest in exotic places on their 1868 trip to Egypt and she wished to know more about the Empire. She was never able to get over her regret, especially when her son and daughter-in-law and later her grandson travelled to India. Alexandra, not

Alexandra's arrival at Gravesend to marry the Prince of Wales was the occasion for great celebrations. Painting by Henry Nelson O'Neil.

being a reader, learned by meeting people and her charm attracted the great men of the day such as Tennyson. She was particularly fond of games and practical jokes and gatherings at Marlborough House and Sandringham were noted for their informality. Yet contemporaries always remarked that one never forgot that Alexandra was the Princess of Wales and she could maintain her dignity in the most ridiculous situations.

It has been said that Queen Victoria was the grandmother of the royal houses of Europe and that King Christian IX of Denmark was their grandfather. By the time Edward VII died in 1910 Queen Alexandra's originally unprepossessing family had produced royal connections that included her son King George V, her brother King Frederick VIII of Denmark, another brother King George I (Willy) of Greece, her nephew Emperor Nicholas II of Russia and her daughter Maud, Queen Consort to her nephew King Haakon VII (Charles) of Norway. It is not surprising therefore that throughout her life she was interested in foreign affairs, though it was a family interest rather than a political one – an extension of her domestic life. Queen Victoria had forseen difficulties in the Prince of Wales marrying a Danish princess, "the young Prin-

cess must put strong Danish feelings, if she has any, in her pocket". This Alexandra was never able to do though she was always British first.

There was no question of the Princess seriously interfering in political affairs but her hatred of Prussia was well-known and influenced others. The Prince of Wales had been somewhat pro-Prussian before his marriage and changed afterwards. His suspicions of Germany never left him and certainly coloured his view of European affairs. But it would be difficult to judge the degree this was the influence of Alexandra. Edward had become a francophile early in his life when he visited the Emperor Napoleon III as a child and the animosity between the two great continental powers was more significant than the role of Denmark. The absorption of Hanover by Prussia in 1866 did not endear Germany to the royal family either. Finally there was Edward's personal dislike of his nephew Kaiser Wilhelm and Britain's natural fear of any European power growing too strong. Alexandra probably reinforced tendencies that were already there.

The Danish-Prussian war over Schleswig-Holstein broke out in December 1863 and after a pause was revived in the spring, a week after Prince Eddy's

60

Edward, Prince of Wales. Chalk drawing by G. F. Watts.

The three daughters of Alexandra, Louise, Victoria and Maud, though not unattractive, suffered from continual comparison with their beautiful mother. S. P. Hall's oil painting 1883.

birth. Alexandra's distress delayed her recovery and the British public rallied to the Danish side in a demonstration of Alexandra's personal appeal.

British policy, though, was to remain neutral and Denmark was defeated. Alexandra was never reconciled with Germany. In 1890, Prince George accompanied his father on a tour of Germany and was made an honorary colonel of a German regiment. Alexandra wrote to him "my Georgie boy has become a real, live, filthy, blue-coated, picklehaube German soldier!!!" adding maternally, "It was your misfortune, not your fault".

But Alexandra was not always blindly irrational about Germany though. That same year Britain considered trading Heligoland, acquired from Denmark in 1814, to Germany for Zanzibar. In a memorandum to Lord Roseberry she quite eloquently showed why the transaction was against Britain's interests – that Heligoland dominated the German coast and would be important for both sides in the event of war. She was not heeded and Heligoland was turned over, yet some historians believe World War I proved her right. In 1863 Alexandra's brother Willy became King George I of Greece on the recommendation of the British government and this began her absorbing interest in Balkan affairs, motivated by her point that "England

put my brother there and are bound to keep him there". Tragically Willy was assassinated in 1913. Domestically Alexandra and Edward might have changed Irish history had they been allowed their way. In 1868 they made their first trip to Ireland and achieved an immediate rapport with the people. Alexandra wore a dress of Irish poplin and a mantilla of Irish lace while Edward wore a green tie and shamrock. The Queen was against Alexandra going so soon after her illness, and security concerns were legitimate in light of the Fenian troubles.

Alexandra insisted however and it was 1863 all over. *The Times* referred to "The Danish Conquest of Ireland" as the Irish found the Princess with her charm, beauty and emotional nature to be one of them. At Phoenix Park in Dublin a voice called out from the crowd "we'll never let her leave us, and if she's here the Prince will have to stay too". In fact the Prince and Princess wanted to establish a permanent residence in Ireland and live there for part of the year or even become viceroy and vicereine. They had realized the need for the royal family to be actually present and Alexandra even suggested the Queen should visit Ireland. Alexandra was also motivated by the fact that she personally preferred Ireland to Scotland where the Queen expected her family to join her

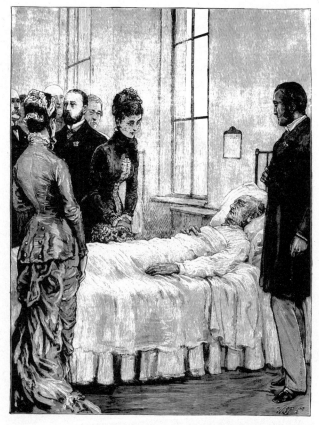

Some roles of a Princess of Wales have not changed in a century. (Right) Alexandra plants a tree in Abbey Park, Leicester, 1882 and (left) visits Marylebone Infirmary, 1881.

regularly. Edward and Alexandra may not have been politically astute, they were still in their twenties, but their instinctive understanding of people told them what was needed. And a non-English British princess might have been just right in Ireland. But the Queen would not listen despite the favourable opinion of both Disraeli and Gladstone and the great opportunity was lost. When Victoria did finally go back to Ireland in 1900, after thirty-nine years, it was too late.

Alexandra's religious beliefs demonstrated both her ability to think for herself and her devotion to a principle. She had been raised in Denmark as a Lutheran, also the historic faith of the Hanoverians and Queen Victoria was a strong Protestant. The Prince of Wales, despite his reputation, also was a religious man and a regular church-goer in his later life. But in the couple's early years of marriage, the Queen thought they were too casual about religion and complained about it. After the Prince's near fatal attack of typhoid in November 1871 they promised to reform, which pleased the Queen, and they became Anglo-Catholics attending the highest of all high churches, All Saints, Margaret Street, which was not what Victoria had in mind. The Prince and Princess had in fact been introduced to the Oxford Movement through friends of the Prince early in their marriage.

The Queen's objections led to a compromise by which the Princess, whose views were stronger than Edward's, attended the Chapel Royal on Sunday morning and All Saints for evensong and occasionally on weekdays. The degree of her conversion from Lutheranism was shown again in 1890 when she criticised Prince George for receiving communion at a Lutheran service in Germany. "I am really sorry you should have done so, as with you it must have been a perfect farce as you have often told me you could not understand a word of German. How could you suddenly have got so learned to be able to take part in such a sacred ceremony – and although you imagine it is exactly the same as our English service, certainly the forms are different, the doctrine also."

With the death of Queen Victoria on 22 January 1901, Alexandra became Queen Consort, a title which she did not like to use, preferring simply "the Queen". As Queen she continued her interest in charitable organizations and founded the Queen Alexandra Imperial Nursing Service, at her own expense, originally for service in South Africa. Alexandra was still regarded as the most beautiful woman in the land and when she was sixty-four, Margot Asquith could say that the Queen made "every other woman look common beside her".

Edward's death in 1910 after a short reign of only nine years came suddenly and was devastating to Alexandra. Despite his infidelity they were devoted to each other and her personal and official life had revolved around him for fifty years – since as a girl of sixteen destiny chose her as his bride-to-be. She was now adrift, yet in a way content. The funeral was not held for a fortnight as the Queen was reluctant to part with the King's body. Lord Esher described Alexandra in these days as showing "a tenderness which betrayed all the love in her soul, and oh! so natural feeling that she had got him there altogether to herself. In a way she seemed and is, I am convinced, happy".

Alexandra remained actively interested in public affairs during her son King George V's reign and he kept her informed of matters. She regularly wrote to him on Greek and Danish concerns to his tolerant despair but offered sensible words of advice during the parliamentary crisis of 1911. During the world war she devoted herself to war charities and fund raising schemes such as Queen Alexandra's Gift Book. She took a keen interest in her grandchildren, especially in the Prince of Wales' (Edward VIII) tours of India and Canada in 1919. But her deafness became worse and she grew frailer and felt isolated from the world. She spent her time at her beloved Sandringham, regularly attending Sandringham Church and in the company of her old friends and members of her family. She died there on 20 November 1924, ten days before her eightieth birthday.

Alexandra's life was marred by her physical disabilities and pain and so many disappointments, tragedies and failed ambitions. A long apprenticeship for a short reign, an unfaithful husband, two sons who died young, a brother, brother-in-law, nephews, nieces and other relations assassinated in Greece and Russia, a lonely widowhood, failed hopes in Ireland and regrets at not being able to see the Empire were just the most prominent. But she helped lead the monarchy into the twentieth century and made it popular with the people. She gave it an informal glamour that is still its hallmark and its strength. She produced a son who was not only devoted to her but who had personal qualities, which she helped shape, that made him a great monarch, and a daughter who is still remembered with affection in her adopted kingdom of Norway. Alexandra was a successful princess and queen and a good if imperfect person who made those around her happy. She lived and died with the love of her people, which is no mean epitaph.

Mary of Teck

1867 – 1953

Princess May of Teck the eighth Princess of Wales broke a four-and-a-half century pattern, for though she had a German title, a German father and German ancestors, she was born at Kensington Palace, London on 26 May 1867. This native birth was the key to her startling rise to be the wife of George the nineteenth Prince of Wales. Christened Victoria Mary Augusta Louise Olga Pauline Claudine Agnes, she had Queen Victoria as her godmother and was known as Princess May from the month of her birth. She is best remembered as Queen Mary, a title she held for forty-three years.

May was the only daughter of the Duke and Duchess of Teck. A romantic streak in Princess Alexandra, her predecessor as Princess of Wales, was indirectly responsible for May's existence, but it was because of her mother that she came to be born at historic Kensington. The Duchess of Teck had the more important title of Princess Mary Adelaide of Cambridge, for she was a granddaughter of King George III and thus in line to the throne. Mary Adelaide, or 'Fat Mary' in the family, was a high-spirited woman whose popularity with Londoners made her first cousin, Queen Victoria, jealous. Her marriage prospects were not good since she was poor. In 1865 when she was thirty-two, Albert Edward and Alexandra the recently-married Prince and Princess of Wales, took things in hand for her. They had met

Prince Francis of Teck in Vienna and taken a fancy to the handsome member of the Royal Family of Wurttemberg. Thinking he would be perfect for Mary Adelaide, they invited him across the channel. Mary Adelaide fell in love and married him.

Though Francis endowed his daughter with artistic tastes and intellectual interests he had little else to offer. Life was permanently spoiled for him because he could never succeed to the Wurttemberg throne. Francis' mother the beautiful Countess Claudia Rhedey of Kis Rede, a Hungarian from Transylvania, had not been a princess and her children had no dynastic rights. Even being created Duke of Teck on his marriage never reconciled Francis to the morganatic status of his family.

Since the Prince and Princess of Wales had engineered the Teck marriage, the two families were close and May shared the childhood of her future husband Prince George. May grew up at White Lodge, a small country house in Richmond Park, but paid frequent visits to relatives in Germany and Austria. Though beset by family problems her childhood was happy and she was reared carefully and strictly. One cousin remembered her as a tomboy.

May's mother who ran public charities successfully could not live within her income. Persistent worries over her extravagance added to the restlessness of May's father who had not been given any official

Engagement picture of May and Prince Albert Victor, Duke of Clarence and Avondale.

As Princess of Wales about 1906.

work to do by Queen Victoria and in idleness fretted over questions of rank. Financial affairs reached a crisis in 1883 and the Tecks had to retire to a villa in Florence. They travelled under the name of Hohenstein. May was acutely embarrassed by the ridiculous appearance she felt they made, all talking and looking English but signing a German name.

May had already learned dancing from Taglioni and spoke German and French but her real education began in Florence. She studied French and Italian literature, visited the city's famous museums, galleries and churches and acquired the technique of learning. For her age she showed exceptional discretion, firmness and tact and was peacemaker in the family between parents and among three brothers. Even her mother's extravagance and unpunctuality had taught her to be frugal and business-like. Her aunt, the formidable old Grand Duchess Augusta of Mecklenberg-Strelitz, instilled pride in her descent from the Royal Family.

She was now a young woman of average height with fair hair, piercing blue eyes and a soft voice who carried herself gracefully and had a grave and alert expression which hinted at a desire to be amused. But how did she come to marry the Heir Presumptive to the British throne? After all her lack of fortune meant she could not expect to marry a British nobleman and her morganatic blood prevented her being sought as consort by even a minor German prince. The answer lay with the Royal Family.

Queen Victoria changed her mind about Princess May at this time. Till now the Queen had kept the Tecks, with their money worries and social ambitions at a distance. But as soon as May's personality had a chance to make itself felt, Queen Victoria came to like her. The Queen had always regarded the German aversion to morganatic blood as foolish. Concern was growing in the Royal Family about Prince Albert Victor of Wales, Duke of Clarence and Avondale, son of the Prince of Wales and second in line to the Throne. Known as "Eddy" the tall young prince with gentle eyes had considerable charm but was listless, wayward and volatile. Periods at sea, at Cambridge University and in the 10th Hussars had not improved him. Recent wild suggestion has cast him as Jack the Ripper but it's likely he was simply a late developer.

Prince Eddy's parents, the Prince and Princess of Wales, and the Queen decided that the answer was for him to marry a strong-minded princess who would guide him to maturity and coax him out of his intellectual lethargy. Eddy agreed but promptly fell in love with a French princess whom he could not marry because of her religion. It did not take long for the Royal Family to hit upon the obvious choice close at hand — Princess May. May herself was unaware of these plans but in November 1891 she was summoned to Balmoral for a ten day visit. The following month at Luton Hoo, a Bedfordshire country house, Albert Victor proposed to her and May accepted him.

She did not know her cousin well and was not in love with him, but her personal feeling for the monarchy left her in no doubt about the great honour of being asked to marry the future king. In her heart she believed she could fulfil the role expected of her. Since she did not have a passionate nature she was content to try to love Prince Eddy after they were married. The months of their engagement did bring doubts as she began to know him better. Despite these, she would still have married him had an attack of influenza not caused Eddy to die suddenly at Sandringham on 14 January 1892.

Shock gripped the nation because May's engagement had been popular. The press began openly talking about her marrying Eddy's younger brother Prince George, and the idea appealed to the Royal Family. May's sensitive nature found such an idea repulsive and she soon fled to the south of France. The idea did not appeal to Prince George either who felt he was too young to marry. But this shy, bluff young man, honest and eager to do his duty, before long bowed to his family's wishes and on 3 May 1893 proposed to May in the garden of Sheen Lodge near London. May having had time to overcome her initial revulsion accepted him. Though she was not any more passionately in love with George than she had been with his brother, she liked him and their mutual grief for Eddy drew them together. The wedding took place at the Chapel Royal, St. James's Palace two months later on 6 July. For their honeymoon they went to Sandringham and moved into York Cottage, the royal estate's small bachelors' quarters which was to be their home for thirty-three years.

May now Duchess of York found it difficult to live so close to the Prince and Princess of Wales. She felt isolated and lacked independence; even York Cottage had been decorated without reference to her wishes. In the closely knit, sentimental world of her husband and his sisters, whose education had been narrow and inferior to that of the Tecks, there was no outlet for May's intellectual interests. She found her father-in-law awesome and Princess Alexandra, who was jealous of her, eccentric and trying. May managed to cope with these problems without giving way to unpleasantness or bitterness and while the effort made her more reserved it gained her the grateful love of her husband.

At first the public role played by May and George was limited and May was able to bear her first three children in comparative peace. Edward, the future Duke of Windsor was born in 1894, the future George

May with her three eldest children, the future Edward VIII (left), future George VI (right) and Mary future Princess Royal.

VI in 1895 and Princess Mary in 1897. The Duke and Duchess took part in the Diamond Jubilee and made successful visits to Ireland in 1897 and 1899 but not until the Boer War broke out did their official engagements markedly increase.

The history of the modern Princesses of Wales is one of an ever expanding Commonwealth role. Princess Alexandra had not been allowed to accompany the Prince of Wales to India in 1875, much as she wished to, but May made a real breakthrough. When Queen Victoria decided to send George to open the first Parliament of the new Commonwealth of Australia, May was determined not to miss such an opportunity even if it meant braving the sea-sickness she dreaded and always suffered. Now, she went as Duchess of Cornwall and of York. Queen Victoria had ended her epic reign in January 1901 and the Prince of Wales had become King. But George and May had not yet become Prince and Princess of Wales. The new King and Queen had held this title so long that Edward VII wished a period to elapse before bestowing it on his son and daughter-in-law to avoid confusion. George meanwhile as heir had automatically inherited the Duchy of Cornwall.

They sailed on 16 March 1901 by way of Port Said and Ceylon. After the Duke opened Parliament in

King George v. Oil painting by Whiting.

Marlborough House was May's official London residence as Princess of Wales.

Banner embroidered by May as Princess of Wales and presented to Villa Maria School, Montreal.

Shooting the timber slides of the Chaudière during the 1901 tour of Canada.

Flowers and gold and silver are scattered before Princess May as she enters Bombay City Hall during the visit to India.

Melbourne on 9 May, he and May visited Brisbane and Sydney, journeyed to New Zealand and returned via Tasmania and Adelaide. From Australia they went to South Africa where war was still raging, leaving Cape Town on 23 August and reaching Quebec on 16 September. A splendid train decorated in Louis XV style took them across Canada and back again. May worked hard to make the tour a success and unconsciously shed her shyness, at least momentarily. It came as a surprise to her that she was popular wherever they went because in the Prince of Wales' circle she had been voted dull.

When they returned Edward VII rewarded his son by creating him Prince of Wales on 9 November 1901. May was now Princess of Wales. What role would she make for herself? She and her husband soon found that once again they would not have a great share of the royal duties because the King, so long deprived of serious work, intended to do everything himself. In other respects the pattern of May's life was quickly settled. She moved into Marlborough House, which was to be their London residence and a maturer George handed its decoration over to her. Abergeldie on the River Dee, a medieval tower with walled garden near Balmoral was their Scottish home. But May most appreciated the King's gift of Frogmore House in Windsor Home Park because she loved to use it as a retreat from the hectic life of London.

May's three youngest children were born to her as Princess of Wales. Prince Henry, future Duke of Gloucester, had been born in 1900 and he was followed in 1902 by Prince George, who became Duke of Kent, and in 1905 by Prince John. The peevish tone of the memoirs of her first son, the Duke of Windsor, has led May and George to be judged harshly as parents. In fact they were affected by contemporary attitudes to children but often rose above them. May was not generous with her caresses but she liked children, devoted a special hour each evening to them and took them on many carriage drives and picnic teas. George was more severe and shyer in his relations with his children. Their real failure was in the education of their eldest sons David and Bertie. Princes it was still thought could not go to school, so George and May attempted to reproduce the schoolroom at home. Without other children this could not work and it left permanent scars on David and Bertie. Realising this failure the Prince and Princess later sent their younger sons to school.

Being Princess of Wales took May on foreign state visits. In April 1904 she and George went to see the venerable Austrian Emperor Francis Joseph and May captivated the punctilious Habsburg court with her fluent German, ease and charm of manner. The Prince had never mastered German and without his wife's presence would have found the visit an ordeal. From Vienna they went to Wurttemberg where May watched her husband confer the Order of the Garter on King William II, head of the royal house that would acknowledge her only as a morganatic member. When bombs were thrown during King Alfonso XIII's wedding in Madrid two years later, killing and wounding many, May's self-possession was widely commended. She took her daughter Princess Mary along to the cornation of her sister-in-law and brother-in-law as King and Queen of Norway at Trondheim and in 1908 there were visits to Darmstadt and Paris.

In 1905 the Prince and Princess of Wales set out on a tour of India. May prepared for months ahead, reading extensively about local history, geography and customs. The exotic beauty of India fascinated her and when she returned the following year she had not only experienced the splendour of Indian princely life but had gone incognito into the streets of Indian cities to see the homes of the poor. A third Empire tour planned for August 1910 had to be cancelled because of the accession of George and May to the Throne. Each of these visits built new relationships. After the tour of Canada May sent banners she had hand embroidered to the nuns at Villa Maria School in Montreal and to Toronto and McGill Universities.

During these nine years May laid the foundation of her famous collections. When her uncle, the Duke of Cambridge, died in 1904 many of his possessions were dispersed and May worked hard to track them down. Her slim resources made this difficult but Lord and Lady Mount Stephen helped her. Lady Mount Stephen was an old Teck friend and her husband, a builder of the Canadian Pacific Railway. Together they bought items May could not afford and helped catalogue them, assuring the preservation of much eighteenth and nineteenth century royal history in the form of portraits, furniture, china and silver. May also carried on and expanded her mother's charity work. Of special interest to her was the London Needlework Guild which became known as Queen Mary's Needlework Guild. She regularly and professionally sorted and packed many thousands of garments made by its members and tackled the huge task of distributing them.

May's life as Princess of Wales ended abruptly and unexpectedly on 6 May 1910 when the King died. The Prince was proclaimed King George V and May became Queen consort. Allowing for today's enlarged field of activity, her role had been more like that of Diana the present Princess of Wales than of any Princess of the past. These years had given May the personal confidence she needed to enable her to make the supreme effort of being Queen from 1910 to 1936. As the Royal Family had originally hoped, she had

helped her husband, (but George and not Albert Victor) to mature. Leading him through deeper and wider reading to make up the deficiencies in his education and to develop his faculties, May was one of the influences that made George V one of the most effective of our constitutional monarchs. She also had the personal satisfaction of having inspired him with a deep love for her.

She would have preferred a longer apprenticeship but what she had was sufficient to allow her to face the shocks and setbacks she had to endure as Queen Mary. Her youngest son Prince John was to die at thirteen from epilepsy in 1919 and Prince George the Duke of Kent to perish in an air crash while on active service in 1942. She was called on to give a supreme example of moral leadership when World War I gripped the Empire in a life and death struggle and brought down the monarchial order of Europe. After losing her husband she was to have the added sorrow of the abdication of her eldest son King Edward VIII who forsook the principles of duty she lived by. At that grave crisis she stepped forward as head of the family. The satisfaction of watching her next son, George VI, take up the cause of duty would be tempered by the sadness of having him die early as a result. Queen Mary lived on into her eighty-sixth year and died at Marlborough House on 24 March 1953.

A popular idea of the Princess of Wales and her work for the Needlework Guild.

Lady Diana Spencer

1961

Probably more has been recorded about the ninth Princess of Wales than was committed to paper on all her predecessors combined — and her life has scarcely begun. She is the first to feel, personally, the full effect of jet travel, satellite communication, television and the telephoto lens. All this new technology has its good and bad side-effects.

On one hand, royal tours are not the highly orchestrated, lengthy and exhausting cavalcades by ship and rail of the past. Now it is possible for royalty to drop in for a few days, and the pressure is less. People know, when a royal comes, that this is not a once-in-a-lifetime opportunity, not to be missed. On the other hand, technology has made it almost impossible for royalty to preserve any privacy.

Reporters and photographers from all the news media dog the footsteps of the royals. Those from certain Fleet Street tabloids are particularly offensive in their harrassment of the royal family, as they seek to catch a royal in an awkward moment. Failing that, a front page photograph of a more conventional sort, accompanied by a sensational headline, is guaranteed to sell out an edition. None suffer more from the dubious Fleet Street motto — "Make it fast, make it early, make it up" — than the members of the royal family.

From the moment in 1980 when the hounds scented that the Prince of Wales was seeing a nineteen year-old, part-time kindergarten teacher named Lady Diana Spencer, the hunt was on. The speculation was not new. The merest hint that Prince Charles was seeing any woman was enough to launch the furor. The real turning point came on 24 February 1981, when the official announcement of the engagement was made. Overnight Lady Diana Spencer became one of the most famous women in the world. That she has style, is extremely attractive, are bonuses, as is the Prince's choice of an Englishwoman, the first since Lady Anne Neville, the second Princess of Wales, 500 years ago. Even Mary of Teck, although born in England, had a German title and fitted the tradition of the heir to the throne marrying into one of Europe's royal families.

Much else has changed since Mary of Teck was Princess of Wales. Members of the royal family are more casual, but, aware of the need to maintain some dignity, rely on customs of the past and are careful not to be too informal. Prince Charles, an avowed traditionalist, has learned to have an easy rapport with the people he meets, and having grown up in the face of publicity, knows how to avoid being led into expressing opinions that might be controversial. Today's monarchy would not endure long without the good will of the people.

For Lady Diana, living in the royal goldfish bowl is a new and at times exasperating experience. She

Diana as a baby in her pram at Park House, Sandringham where her early years were spent.

At age 9 playing croquet.

was one of many Englishwomen who have titles, but who, unless they do something outstanding or outrageous, attract little attention. Yet she was as well prepared for the position she holds as consort to the Prince of Wales as any woman could be. Most European princesses lead fairly conventional lives, noticed occasionally by the international press. Lady Diana's family is British, wealthy, upper class, titled, the sort that mingles with members of the royal family, and from which the public expected the future Princess of Wales to come. Once the engagement was official, Buckingham Palace stood by ready to make the transition from an obscure young noblewoman to a celebrity as painless as possible.

She was born, in the room where her mother had been born twenty-five years before, on 1 July 1961, as the Honourable Diana Spencer. She is the third child of John Viscount Althorp and the Honourable Frances Roche. Diana's father was heir to Albert Edward John 7th Earl Spencer (a godson of Edward VII). Her mother is a daughter of the late Maurice 4th Lord Fermoy, who died in 1953, and of Ruth Gill Lady Fermoy. Like the Queen Mother, Lady Fermoy is a Scotswoman, and the two are friends of long standing.

The Spencer and Roche families' association with the royal family traces back many centuries. Although the 1st Earl Spencer's title was conferred in 1765, during the reign of George III, the Spencers descend from Henry VII and his Queen Elizabeth through their daughter, Princess Mary the Dowager Queen of France, who later married Charles Brandon Duke of Suffolk. A daughter of Mary and Charles, Lady Frances Brandon, married Henry Grey, who succeeded his father-in-law as Duke of Suffolk. Their daughters were Lady Jane and Lady Katherine Grey. Lady Jane Grey was made the heir to the dying Edward VI. In 1553, after a reign of nine days, she was deposed by Katharine of Aragon's daughter, Mary I, and in 1554 beheaded. The 1st Earl Spencer was descended from Lady Katherine Grey.

The present Princess of Wales' paternal grandmother was Lady Cynthia Hamilton Countess Spencer, who died in 1972. She was a Lady in Waiting to the Queen Mother, as was Diana's maternal grandmother, Lady Fermoy, until she retired in 1981. The Hamiltons descend from James II of Scotland through his daughter Mary, and one of them was once heir presumptive to Mary Queen of Scots (the mother of James VI of Scotland and I of England). Through her father, Diana inherited some interesting royal blood. She is twelfth in descent from King Henri IV of France who founded the Bourbon dynasty and sent Samuel de Champlain to Canada as the first governor. Her son Prince William is therefore the first heir to the Throne of Canada descended from both the Hanoverian and

Bourbon houses which ruled Canada.

Her mother's family, the Roche family is of Anglo-Irish origin and has been traced back to the reign of Edward IV. The barony of Fermoy was conferred by Queen Victoria in 1856, but the title existed much earlier. Lady Diana's mother descends from a branch that first came to prominence in the reign of Elizabeth I. Their estate, Trabolgan, in County Cork, Ireland, was sold in 1880.

The other children in the Spencer family were the Honourable Sarah, born in 1955, the Honourable Jane in 1957, and the Honourable Charles, the youngest in 1964. They lived in rambling Park House, on the Sandringham estate in Norfolk, which the 4th Lord Fermoy had leased from the Crown, and which lease Diana's father took over when Lady Fermoy, Diana's grandmother, wanted a smaller home. As in most wealthy British families, the Spencer children had a governess, Miss Gertrude Allen, nicknamed "Ally", who had also been governess to their mother. They received their first lessons at home and then at a local day school before being sent to boarding school, very much the same start as the Queen and Prince Philip agreed on for their own four children.

When Diana was six years old her parents separated, and in 1969 they were divorced, by which time Diana was eight. That same year her mother married Mr. Peter Shand Kydd of Ardencaple, Isle of Seil, near Oban, Scotland. The Spencer children remained at Park House in the custody of their father. Divorce and step-parents are traumatic experiences for young children, and Lady Fermoy did her best to help her grandchildren through that difficult time.

Diana's preparatory school, where she went at age seven and stayed three years, was Riddlesworth Hall, in Diss, Norfolk, not far from Park House. She is remembered as not academically inclined, but very nice to the younger girls. Next she was sent to a girl's public school, West Heath, near Sevenoaks, Kent. During their school years the Spencer children became acquainted with the royal children. Princes Andrew and Edward were close in age to Diana and her brother Charles, while the older girls, Sarah and Jane, were compatible with Prince Charles and Princess Anne. When the royal family spent the usual holiday at Sandringham in January, the younger members enjoyed the companionship of the young Spencers. Diana, nearly thirteen years younger than Charles, certainly saw him in those years, but did not get to know him until later. (The suggestion that he married "the girl next door" is somewhat of an exaggeration).

In 1975 Diana's grandfather died and her father became the 8th Earl Spencer. The family moved to the ancestral home, Althorp, in Northamptonshire. The

Lord Snowden's engagement study of the Prince of Wales and Lady Diana Spencer.

three Spencer sisters became Ladies Sarah, Jane and Diana, their brother Charles succeeded their father as Viscount Althorp. The following year Earl Spencer married Raine, the former wife of the Earl of Dartmouth and daughter of the romantic novelist Barbara Cartland. By the time her father remarried, Lady Diana was on good terms with her mother. Part of her school holidays she spent at the Shand Kydd farmhouse on the Isle of Seil, or at the flat her mother kept in Cadogan Place, London.

In January 1978 Diana left West Heath and spent two terms at a finishing school in Switzerland, the Institut Alpin Videmanette, near Gstaad. She decided not to return to work further towards her "A" level examinations since she did not plan on going to a university. Instead she went to London, to do the things she loved, cooking, homemaking, being involved with small children, and seeing a circle of good friends. Her parents bought her a flat in Coleherne Court, on the Brompton Road, which she shared with three other girls — Virginia Pitman, a friend from West Heath, music student Caroline Pride, and Anne Bolton. Lady Diana was a part-time cook and a nanny, before becoming a volunteer teacher at the Young England Kindergarten, a private school in Pimlico.

In November 1977, during Lady Diana's last term at West Heath, Lady Sarah Spencer invited Prince Charles to spend a weekend shooting at Althorp. Sixteen year-old Lady Diana was there, now developing into a tall young woman, mature for her years,

Arriving in open carriage for Diana's first Ascot as a member of the royal party.

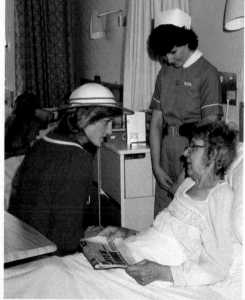

Chat with a patient at Royal Preston Hospital in Lancashire, June 1983.

Ayers Rock, a famous Australian landmark, forms a background for the Prince and Princess.

Surrounded by an admiring crowd at the Terry Fox Centre, Ottawa.

with excellent dress sense and a fine complexion. This was a beginning, but some time passed before the Prince of Wales became seriously interested in her.

Following her return from Switzerland in the summer of 1978, while living in London, she spent most weekends at Althorp and her summers in Scotland. She was invited several times to Balmoral Castle, where the royal family goes every year towards the end of August, but she was considered a friend of Prince Andrew. Prince Charles was there, but he had his own friends and they were preoccupied with shooting and fishing.

In 1980 Lady Diana was a guest of the royal family for Cowes Week, the annual regatta off the Isle of Wight, when she stayed aboard the royal yacht *Britannia*. Again she was invited to Balmoral, and this time Prince Charles asked her to join him on his fishing expeditions along the River Dee. On Sunday, 7 September, a photographer spotted the couple fishing and the game was up. On Monday the Prince's latest romance made headlines.

Next, Lady Diana was present at the Prince's birthday party on 14 November. The following January she spent three days with the royal family at

Highgrove House, Gloucestershire, home of Diana and Charles which the Prince acquired in 1980.

Sandringham. About that time the Prince proposed and asked her to think over his offer. He went skiing in Switzerland, while in London Lady Diana fielded reporters' questions, managing to be gracious as they followed her and waited at the entrance to her flat. Her mother was in Australia, where she owns a sheep station in New South Wales, and Diana decided to visit her.

On her return she accepted the Prince's proposal, and she left her flat to take up residence in Clarence House, the home of the Queen Mother. There she could keep reporters at arm's length, while being eased into the complexities of living as a royal. With her way of tilting her head and looking out from under her eyelashes, the press soon nicknamed her "Shy Di". Not so, Palace spokesmen have since maintained. She is five feet ten and one half inches tall, and a little self-conscious about her height. Tilting her head was a way of appearing shorter until she realized that holding it high made her look more striking, even though her head was on a level with her husband's.

The wedding was set for 29 July 1981. Prince Charles chose St. Paul's Cathedral rather than Westminster Abbey because the fine accoustics would enhance the music he wanted played. Lady Diana concurred. St. Paul's was larger and would hold more guests, and for her Westminster Abbey had unhappy associations. Her parents' unsuccessful marriage had been solemnized there.

The ceremony, staged with all the pomp and majesty at which the royal family excels, was seen by millions throughout the world. The service, at ten o'clock in the morning London time, reached early risers in Toronto, Canada, five hours earlier, while viewers in Perth, Australia, watched it at five o'clock in the afternoon. This was the first royal wedding held at St. Paul's since that of Arthur Prince of Wales and Katharine of Aragon, in November 1501, although the buildings were different. Old St. Paul's was burnt in the Great Fire of London in 1666, when the tomb of John of Gaunt was destroyed.

The Prince and Princess of Wales began their honeymoon at Broadlands, the home of the Prince's great uncle, the late Lord Mountbatten, where his parents had also started their honeymoon. Then the couple went on a cruise in the Mediterranian aboard the royal yacht *Britannia*, finishing at Balmoral Castle where the other members of the royal family were on holiday. The London home of the Prince and Princess is a suite of nine rooms in Kensington Palace. As well they have a country home, Highgrove, a rolling estate in Gloucestershire, in the lovely Cotswold country. Highgrove is a mile north of Tetbury, and about two hours' drive from London. Bought by the Duchy of Cornwall for the Prince in 1980, it is not far from

Gatcombe Park, the home of Princess Anne and her husband, Mark Phillips.

On November 5, not long after a successful visit to Wales, the Palace announced that the Princess of Wales was expecting a baby in June. Projected tours of Australia, New Zealand and Canada had to be postponed. In February 1982, Charles and Diana took a holiday on the Island of Windermere, in the Bahamas. Of course the press would not let them alone, and a photographer using a zoom lens stole a shot of the pregnant Princess in a bikini. Newspapers ran the photograph, and loud protests followed. Certain of the tabloids apologized, publishing the photograph again along with protestations of respect for the Princess. Despite all the furor the photograph was not unflattering.

In the past ladies of the royal family ceased appearing in public when their pregnancies were advanced. Diana blossomed forth in stylish maternity wear and continued making public appearances until six days before the birth of Prince William of Wales. The Prince and Princess departed from tradition in having their baby born in a hospital, St. Mary's Paddington, rather than in a specially prepared suite at home. On 21 June 1982, the Prince was in the delivery room to witness the birth of his son — all very up to date.

From the earliest days of the press, of scurrilous pamphlets and just old fashioned gossips, the private affairs of the royal family have made good copy, often erroneously reported. Just as stories of the supposed affair between Augusta the fifth Princess of Wales and Lord Bute were without foundation but widely accepted, so the present Prince and Princess of Wales are victimized, for a mere hint of difficulties between them is blown up out of all proportion. At the slightest flicker of impatience the Fleet Street hacks gleefully report that the marriage is in trouble. How aggravating that must be, always on guard lest even trusted friends or servants under oath talk out of turn.

In 1983 the Prince and Princess carried out the postponed tours of Australia, New Zealand and Canada. Anyone watching the Princess, chatting as comfortably to people as the more experienced Prince, realized that here was a remarkable young woman, poised, and for her age, sure of herself. During the Canadian tour, some British journalists claimed that while visiting the eastern Maritime provinces, the royal couple looked bored. How could a couple be bored when seeing new places, surrounded by throngs of adoring spectators, shouting their welcomes?

While British journalists decided that Canadians are boring, Canadian fashion designers complained that the Princess of Wales' wardrobe suited someone older. They were being as nit-picking as the journalists. Most people who see the Princess think she looks stunning. What does matter is how she will handle her role, and the place she will make for herself. The Queen Mother, who started life as Lady Elizabeth Bowes Lyon, also the daughter of an earl, has been one of the best loved members of the royal family.

Being a Princess of Wales has always meant much more than being a wife and mother. None of Lady Diana's predecessors found life that simple and straightforward. The present Princess of Wales has embarked upon a career at the same age as most women of her generation are deciding how they will shape their lives. For women of the western world especially, the possibilities of having a profession, marriage, or a combination of both, have never looked brighter. For the ninth Princess of Wales, one thing is assured; she has one of the most unusual careers in the world today. She has made a resounding beginning.

At Government House, Ottawa, June 1983.

Prince William's first royal tour. The Prince and Princess of Wales pose with their young son in the grounds of Government House, Auckland, New Zealand.